National Lampoon®

A
DIRTY
BOOK

SIGNET Books You'll Enjoy

National Lampoon®

A DIRTY BOOK

EDITED AND WITH AN
INTRODUCTION BY
P. J. O'ROURKE

A SIGNET BOOK from
NEW AMERICAN LIBRARY
TIMES MIRROR

Published by
THE NEW AMERICAN LIBRARY
OF CANADA LIMITED

Copyright © 1976 by National Lampoon, Inc., 635 Madison Avenue, New York, New York 10022.

Published by arrangement with National Lampoon, Inc.

From *National Lampoon*® Magazine: "National Lampoon" is a registered trademark of National Lampoon, Inc. The Lampoon name is used with the permission of the Harvard Lampoon, Inc. Copyright © 1970, 1972, 1973, 1974, 1975, 1976, National Lampoon, Inc., 635 Madison Avenue, New York, New York 10022.

First Printing, March, 1976

1 2 3 4 5 6 7 8 9

For
Reverend A. Day

Contents

Introduction

For the most part, humor writing is a dreary matter of amusing the unfortunate masses by abusing those even less fortunate than they. And this slim assemblage of sophomoricisms regarding man's less attractive biological urges is no exception. Indeed, it would seem to mark a bathosphere depth record in the *National Lampoon*'s continuing attempt to descend to the level of its readers. Jesus, you know you people will buy *anything*. You really will. How do you live with yourselves? I mean, aren't you ashamed? How can you look yourself in the face when you shave? Or, in the case of our distaff audience, how can you look yourself in the armpit? But, listen, I *know* . . . I *know* . . . *I* should talk! Just because I make more money than you'll ever see by randomly dictating this nonsense to my expensive private secretary is no reason why I shouldn't find a less morally reprehensible form of employment, like narcotics informer, for instance, or Republican city councilman. I agree completely. But at least I don't *read* the stuff. Bad enough I have to write it. You don't think I'd actually keep this publication in my home? Volumes of H. H. Munro, Anthony Trollope, and Hugh Walpole, that's what I keep in *my* home. Plus an incredibly svelte and well-dressed girl friend who, despite the constant entreaties of *Vogue* and *Harper's Bazaar*, absolutely refuses to model professionally until Congress puts some teeth in fashion law* and Margaux Hemingway gets life without parole. Her name is Lani. Say hello to the funny-looking readers, Lani. Oh, go ahead. . . . Nope, sorry. She doesn't want any part of you.

But I digress. Where was I, anyway? I seem to remember

---

* Thanks to George W. S. Trow for this appealing concept. George writes for the justifiably prestigious *New Yorker,* and he is a dear friend of mine. Unfortunately, as a result of your purchasing this paperback, George will *never* be a dear friend of yours. George thinks civilized people have to draw the line somewhere.

I was baiting you or something. . . . Yes, that's it. That's what I was doing—*actually baiting the reader*. Some think it's a joke, but others know only too well the stigma of being recognized as "one who buys the *National Lampoon*." Not a pretty fate. But what I'd like to know is, what do you kids get out of this trash? What's so funny about excretion and procreative activity, huh? Personally, I don't get it. Every now and then I have to go out and give lectures at the various cow-town colleges where a great majority of our readers seem to have been interned by their parents, and I'll get up there on the podium in Monied-Alumnus Hall, kid the hell out of the Pre-Raphaelite Brotherhood, sling quips in Chaucerian English, and make hilarious puns on the titles of poems by Hilaire Belloc. What do I hear? I hear *nothing*. That's what I hear. *Total silence*. But let me so much as slide a finger up my nostril or mention "cunt farts," and the place breaks up. Is that *really* what you consider funny? *Really and truly?* I mean, *funny* is Evelyn Waugh's novel *Scoop*—when the newspaper magnate Lord Copper has his managing editor Mr. Salter to dinner and afterward, they retire to the library for brandy and Lord Copper says, ". . .

But why waste our time? You're not going to laugh at stories like that. Because if you *did* laugh at stories like that there wouldn't *be* a *National Lampoon*, and I'd be out of a job. I give up:

> Trouser ham
> Slime socket
> Punish the Pope
> Nose oysters
> Fun faucet
> Pink train in the tummy tunnel
> Kiss the carp
> Clam jam
> Drain the snake
> Bum brownies
> Drilling for mud bunnies
> Giggle hose
> Park your leather yatch in Hair Harbor
> Salmon run up Fur Creek
> Split the hamster
> Hide the baby-leg
> Albino pleasure piss
> Hot lunch coming up

Happy hole
Ring down for more mayonnaise

There! That ought to keep you rolling in the aisles long enough for me to run next door for a couple of doubles straight-up and a six-pack chaser.

Ahhhhhh. . . . That's much better. That's much, much better. Yes, no matter how disgusting any *National Lampoon* project is, it always has its little compensations. Like the opportunity to take a couple of pages right up front to say anything you goddamn please. Maybe you've noticed. Now where the hell else do you have a chance to do a thing like that? Negro jokes, for example. I just heard this incredible Negro joke:

Q. How come colored kids are so easy to baby-sit for?
A. You just wet their lips and stick 'em to a wall!

Isn't that *amazing?* God, that joke'd get your ass kicked in any inner city west of Macao! Martin Mull told me that one. I told it to the guys over at *Rolling Stone* and they laughed their asses off, but do you think that joke'll turn up in "Random Notes"? Not a chance. They're a bunch of pussies over there. But here at the *NatLamp,* we can say anything we want. Of course, personally, I prefer Jew jokes. But you know how it is, we're starting to get a lot of sheenies on staff now, and they've always got some brother-in-law or somebody who's a lawyer in the family. Come to think of it, there are a lot of black guys working here, too, nowadays. I wonder if maybe I'm writing myself into a lot of trouble? That's easy, I'll just sign P.J.'s name. He's so drunk all the time he won't know what hit him. Besides, he's an obnoxious son of a bitch.

Let's see now . . . 904 . . . 905 . . . 906 . . . (we were a little short of material for this book, so they told me to write an extra-long introduction. "Any piece of shit you can whip up," they said, "just make it eat some pages"). I think I've got it licked now, so, listen, enjoy yourself. Really, I mean it. You deserve every word.

P. J. O'ROURKE
*Third from the end with the bottle of Paddy's,
Mike's Wander Inn, the Bronx, 1976*

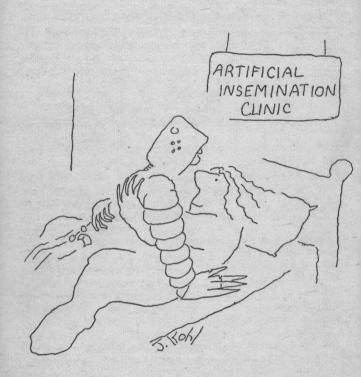

ARTIFICIAL
INSEMINATION
CLINIC

J. Kohl

First Blowjob

*A young girl's senior prom can mean many things:
a bouquet of memories . . . or a pillow full of
tears . . .*

by Doug Kenney

*"Connie! Connie Phillips! You'd better hurry, Jeff will be
here any minute!"*

Mrs. Phillips' call from downstairs found Connie, still in her
freshly ironed slip, sitting crosslegged on the bedspread to put
the finishing touches on her nails. A startled glance at the
clock on the bureau reaffirmed her mother's warning—it was
almost half-past seven. Fanning the air with her hands to dry
the polish, Connie gulped and hurried to dress.

Carefully, she drew the sheer nylons over her tan, athletic
legs and slipped on the white organdy gown that hung in its
plastic bag on her closet door. (Thank heaven Mrs. Phillips
had relented at the store in her preference for the green taffeta
—a high-necked confusion of bows, flounces, and spaghetti
straps that looked more like a circus tent than a party frock.)
Connie fastened the three simple strands of cultured pearls
around her neck and took the rhinestone bracelet Mrs. Phillips
had lent her especially for tonight from the dressing table.
Blotting her cherry-frost lipstick on a tissue and giving her
pert, blond curls one last flick with her brush, Connie sighed
and stepped back from the mirror for final inspection.

Looking at the unfamiliar figure who peered back from the
glass with equally wide-eyed astonishment, Connie suddenly
felt a curious sense of elation. What this afternoon was only
a gum-snapping, floppy-shirted teen with one ear glued to the
telephone and the other permanently cocked toward the hi-fi
had been miraculously transformed—somewhere between this

afternoon's bubble bath and that teetering test-walk in her new yellow satin pumps—into an undeniably attractive, grown-up woman.

Good looks aren't a passport to a happy and productive life, Connie reminded herself as she lingered another moment before the mirror, *but is it wrong to know you're pretty and be glad of it . . . at least for one special night?*

"Hey, nobody told me *Grace Kelly* was in here! I wonder where that dumb old Connie is?"

Connie started from her reverie and quickly flushed with embarrassment as she saw Didi's reflection behind her. Didi Phillips was a pesky, pug-nosed, freckle-faced imp who Connie's parents persisted in maintaining was her own little sister.

"And I suppose no one told you it's impolite to barge into other people's rooms without knocking either?" retorted Connie, whirling around to confront her impudent sibling.

"No-o, but I hear you can get stuck-up from looking at mirrors too long," Didi returned airily. "Anyway, Prince Charming's in the living room getting the Third Degree from Mom an' Pop, so you'd better trot down before he shrivels up like a raisin."

Snatching her handbag from the bureau, Connie brushed by Didi and, pausing at the top of the stairs to take a deep breath, descended in a slow, "ladylike" manner to the living room, where she found Jeff sitting on the couch chatting amiably with her parents. Everyone turned toward Connie as she appeared and Jeff, rising to stand, stared at her with an appreciative grin.

"Ho-ly bananas," exclaimed Jeff, making a comical bow. "I didn't know I had a date with a *movie star!*"

"And *I* didn't know I had a date with such a *smoothie!*" laughed Connie, joining in the general amusement.

"Oh, yes," chuckled Mr. Phillips as he lit his pipe, "Jeff and I have just been discussing that forty-yard pass he made against Hillcrest last season, and now I see why you think he's such a 'dreamboat'!"

For the second time that evening, Connie blushed, then joined Jeff, whose tan, athletic good looks were set off by merry blue eyes and a bow tie in a smart green plaid.

"Now, Wayne," said Mrs. Phillips, "leave the jokes to Jack Benny and let the children go—they don't want to sit around listening to *us.*"

"You're right, Ruth," said Mr. Phillips sheepishly as he knocked the ashes from his pipe and slipped it into the pocket of his cardigan sweater. "You know, it wasn't until you came down those stairs that I realized what a beautiful young woman my little Connie has become."

"Oh, Daddy, don't be silly," chided Connie affectionately as she kissed her father's cheek. "You know I'll *always* be 'your little girl.'"

"I know you will," said Mr. Phillips, "and I also know that Jeff is a fine boy—but there'll be other fine lads around when you go to State in the fall, so I'd like you to promise a pre-historic old dad one thing. . . ."

"Sure, Daddy," said Connie giving a mock conspiratorial wink to Jeff over her father's shoulder, "what is it?"

"Just promise me," said Mr. Phillips, fumbling for his pipe cleaners, "that no matter how wonderful the dance may be tonight, and no matter what Jeff and you may be feeling . . . promise me that you won't give him a blowjob."

"A w-what?" stammered Connie, backing away slightly.

"A blowjob," Mr. Phillips repeated. "You know, when a fellow forces his dork down your throat and makes you suck on it until he eventually shoots his pecker-snot all over your tonsils."

In the silence that followed, Connie, suddenly quite pale, looked beseechingly from Mrs. Phillips to Jeff, both of whom could only avert their eyes to the carpet.

"Oh, my God," gasped Connie, "th-that's . . . horrible . . . *sickening.* . . ."

"You bet it is," replied Mr. Phillips, puffing his pipe alight, "just ask your mother."

Once in Jeff's convertible, Connie tactfully passed over Mr. Phillips' unusual behavior and admired the single, perfect white gardenia Jeff had brought. "What a gorgeous flower," she said as she admired the blossom in Jeff's rear-view mirror, "but you shouldn't have spent so much!"

"Oh, a couple of weekends at hard labor on my pop's lawn mower," Jeff admitted, "but seeing how fabulous you look tonight wearing it makes it a bargain."

"It *is* a grand evening, isn't it?" Connie said, inhaling the fresh late-spring greenery as they sped along Lakeshore Drive to the prom.

"And a grand date for me," Jeff returned. "I feel like the luckiest senior in the history of Parkdale High."

"And *I'm* the luckiest girl," Connie smiled. "After all, it isn't *everybody* who goes to the Spring Bounce with Jeff

Madison—co-captain of the varsity football team, chairman of the Student Senate, *and* Hi-Tri-Y activities coordinator!"

"Aw, cut the soft soap," Jeff laughed. "Let's just say that we're *both* lucky before we get swelled heads!"

"Fun ahoy!" Jeff sang as he turned off Glenview Boulevard into the already crowded parking lot. "Last one on the dance floor is a wallflower!"

"Not me!" cried Connie excitedly. "And you'd better've eaten your Cheerios because I'm not going to sit out a single dance!"

The Senior Bounce was everything Connie hoped it would be, and together with Jeff she floated and swayed to the lilting rhythms of fox-trots, sambas, and polkas until Connie thought her heart would burst.

"I have to powder my nose," said Connie, excusing herself at the break as the crowd eagerly gathered at the tempting tables of Hawaiian Punch and gingersnaps. For Connie it was a perfect evening, or almost perfect, for when Connie went to the coat rack to get a handkerchief from her wrap, she overheard Mary Ellen Peterson and Doris Wilkins whispering by the drinking fountain.

"Doesn't Connie Phillips look ... *sophisticated* tonight?" said Mary Ellen archly.

"Who wouldn't," Doris sniffed, "with that swanky rhinestone bracelet of her mother's?"

"Well," said Mary Ellen, "she certainly seems to have Jeff Madison on a string. Do you think they'll get engaged?"

"Maybe," said Doris vaguely, "although I can't *imagine* Connie not minding Jeff's personality problems ..."

At that point Connie "accidentally" dropped her compact and the two gossips, both red-faced, ended their discussion in mid-meow.

"Hel-lo girls," said Connie. "Did I hear you mention Jeff?"

"W-well, as a matter of fact," began a flustered Mary Ellen, "I was just this minute telling Doris that ... with a *personality* like Jeff's he certainly has no *problem* snagging the most popular girl in Parkdale!"

"Oh," said Connie uncertainly.

The band tuned up again, but this time as Connie whirled around the floor in Jeff's appreciative arms, her happiness was clouded by the snatch of conversation she had overheard in the ladies' room. Even the intoxicating, quicksilver arpeggios of the accordion could not drown out the two false notes in the evening. *Personality problems ... blowjob ... person-*

ality problems ... blowjob, a small, nagging voice kept repeating.

Too soon, the band struck up "Good Night Ladies" and it was time to go. Connie and Jeff were invited to join some of the crowd at the Snak Shoppe for post-prom munchables and, it was darkly hinted, some good-natured hijinx. But Jeff begged off and, as he held Connie's hand, shyly murmured that there was something he wished to ask her alone.

As they drove away under a sky pinpointed with stars, Connie noticed that he was strangely silent. Finally, she asked Jeff if something was troubling him.

"Yes, Connie, there *is* something," Jeff replied as he turned off Lakeshore Drive onto Clinton Avenue. Without a word, he reached into his breast pocket and offered Connie a tiny, velvet-covered box.

She still was staring at the unopened box in her hand when Jeff pulled off Clinton Avenue into a deserted alley next to the Apex Dry Cleaners.

"Oh, Jeff, I don't know what to say," Connie began. "I know we've *talked* about marriage, but I really feel we both should complete our college education at State before I could even *think* of accepting your ring."

Jeff shut off the motor and turned questioningly to Connie. "State . . . marriage . . . ring?" Jeff said puzzledly. *"I'm* not going to State *College.* My folks are sending me to the State *Mental Hospital*—that box I gave you has a couple of Dramamines in it so you don't gag too much when you give me my blowjob."

"Y-your what?" said Connie tonelessly.

"My blowjob," Jeff explained. "You know, where a guy crams his meat into your gullet and you eat on it until he goes spooey all over your uvula."

"Aaah!" Connie screamed, fumbling at the door handle, "No! Jeff, no!" But before she could escape, Connie felt inhumanly powerful hands seize her by the neck and force her head down below the dashboard. There, plainly revealed in the green fluorescent glow of the "Apex" sign, Connie saw Jeff's tan, athletic penis straining toward her.

"Oh, God, please, *no!"* Connie pleaded a last time before Jeff pried her clenching jaws apart with his powerful thumbs and began, by inches, to introduce his swollen flesh past her cherry-frost lipstick. As Jeff plunged and withdrew with pistonlike insistence, Connie felt her glottis constrict involuntarily, seizing the intrusive column.

"Attagirl, Connie," encouraged Jeff, "shake hands with it!"

At last Jeff rose to his final, shuddering spasm and Connie felt a wad of viscous fluid splatter off her palate and slowly began to trickle through her vitals.

"Not bad for a beginner," reassured Jeff as he tied Connie's wrists and ankles to the steering wheel with his matching plaid suspenders. "You should learn to breathe through your nose, though," he added thoughtfully.

When Connie was firmly trussed and secured to the wheel, Jeff excused himself and returned a few moments later wearing a makeshift Nazi uniform, a snapped-off car aerial clutched in his hand.

"Gee," exclaimed Jeff as he began to lash out viciously at her unprotected body, "I've been wanting to try this ever since I first heard Negro music!"

It was many minutes past midnight when a blue convertible screeched to a stop in front of the Phillips' home. A car door could be heard opening, and under the yellow radiance of the streetlight, a limp weight was kicked from the automobile onto the sidewalk before it roared off with a muffled growl.

Slowly, the girl began to stir. Connie, still only semi-conscious, opened her eyes to a brilliant starscape. This puzzled her because she had landed face-first. *Sky up, not down—* Connie reminded herself with the characteristic common sense that had made her one of the most popular seniors at Parkdale, *why stars on ground?* Then, as her eyes began to focus, Connie realized that the twinkling array before her was not stars, but a scattering of precious rhinestones on the pavement.

"Uh-oh, gonna get it now . . ." Connie sang to herself sadly as she crawled across the moist green lawn to her door. Hauling herself to her feet with the aid of a pair of lawn flamingos, Connie used them as simple crutches to stagger the last few steps to the front porch. There, she collapsed and began to scratch feebly at the screen.

Answering the door, Mr. Phillips was surprised to find Connie's crumpled form on the steps, her half-naked body crisscrossed with red welts and her tattered nylons seamed with thin rivulets of dried blood.

"Well, it certainly looks like you've had *your* fun," said Mr. Phillips, "do you have any idea what time it is, young lady?"

10

Connie remained motionless on the steps as Mr. Phillips puffed his pipe angrily. Finally, Mr. Phillips sighed and lifted the dazed girl to her feet and leaned her against the screen door.

"I suppose you think your old dad's an ancient old stick-in-the-mud," said Mr. Phillips. "But I *can* sympathize with the problems facing young people today ... heck, you may not believe it, but I'm even 'hep' to a lot of your kookie teen lingo."

With that, Mr. Phillips' fist struck Connie in the face and sent her somersaulting through the screen door back out onto the lawn, the force of his blow immediately closing her right eye.

"Padiddle, for example," chuckled Mr. Phillips.

"It's hard to believe that even Disneyland has a red-light district."

The Churchill Wit

by Michael O'Donoghue

The celebrated American author Christopher Morley has written, "It's all very easy to become a legend. The difficult thing is not to lose your humanity in doing it." He goes on to conclude that "there are far too many legends and far too few men." Statesman, politician, soldier, orator, sportsman, writer, and amateur artist, in a lifetime that spanned ninety years, Winston Spencer Churchill wore many hats besides the traditional black homburg in which he was so often photographed, and yet the legend never overshadowed the man. Perhaps that is because, whether the fate of nations hung on his words or merely the fate of a dinner party, Sir Winston never lost the precious gift of humor. Just as the history books will record his deeds, we of the National Lampoon would like to recall the wit that tempered those deeds. For is not part of greatness the ability of a man to laugh, not only at himself but, more importantly, at others?

Michael O'Donoghue

Churchill was known to drain a glass or two, and, after one particularly convivial evening, he chanced to encounter a Miss Bessie Braddock, a Socialist member of the House of Commons, who, upon seeing his condition, said, "Winston, you're drunk." Mustering all his dignity, Churchill drew himself up to his full height, cocked an eyebrow, and rejoined, "Shove it up your ass, you ugly cunt."

When the noted playwright George Bernard Shaw sent him two tickets to the opening night of his new play with a note that read, "Bring a friend, if you have one," Churchill, not to be outdone, promptly wired back, "You and your play can go fuck yourselves."

13

Shortly after Churchill had grown a moustache, he was accosted by a certain young lady whose political views were in direct opposition to his own. Fancying herself something of a wag, she exclaimed, "Mr. Churchill, I care for neither your politics nor your moustache."

Unabashed, the young statesman regarded her quietly for a moment, then wryly commented, "Suck my dick."

During the darkest days of World War II, when each night brought waves of Luftwaffe bombers raining death and destruction on a near-defenseless London, Prime Minister Churchill went on the air to address the British people. "I read in this morning's paper that Herr Hitler plans to wring England's neck like that of a chicken," he began, "and I was reminded of what the Irish poacher said as he stood on the gallows. It seems the poor fellow was approached by a well-meaning if somewhat overzealous priest who, in horrific detail, described the unfading torments of Hades which awaited him if he did not repent of his misdeeds. The condemned man listened patiently to all that the priest had to say and, when he was done, grinned broadly and replied, "Eat it raw, fuzz-nuts.""

At an elegant dinner party, Lady Astor once leaned across the table to remark, "If you were my husband, Winston, I'd poison your coffee."

"And if you were my wife, I'd beat the shit out of you," came Churchill's unhesitating retort.

Sir Winston carried on a lifelong feud with Labour Party leader Aneurin Bevan and, on one occasion, while Mr. Bevan was delivering an unusually long speech to the House of Commons, Churchill slumped into his seat and appeared to doze off. When Bevan noticed this, he inquired in his loudest voice, "Must the right honorable gentleman fall asleep during my speech?" Receiving no reply, Mr. Bevan continued until, a few minutes later, the sound of snoring was distinctly audible to all present. This time Mr. Bevan slammed his hand on the rail and fairly shouted, "Until now, the Conservative Party had usually managed to conceal the fact that it was asleep." Without even opening his eyes, Churchill quipped, "Flake off, touch-hole," and unconcernedly resumed his nap.

While serving as a subaltern in the Boer War, the young Churchill was asked by a superior officer to give his opinion of the Boers as soldiers.

"They're assholes, sir," he ventured, then paused briefly and added, with a whimsical smile, "They're assholes."

Churchill was given to reading in the bathtub and, while staying at the White House, he once became so engrossed in an account of the Battle of Fonteney that he forgot President Roosevelt was due to drop by to discuss the upcoming conference in Yalta. At the appointed hour, the President was wheeled into Churchill's quarters only to be informed that the Prime Minister had not finished bathing. Roosevelt was about to apologize for the intrusion and depart when Churchill, puffing his customary cigar, strode into the room stark naked and greeted the nonplussed world leader with a terse, "What are you staring at, homo?"

S. GROSS

Letter to the Editor of Ms. Magazine

by Terry Southern

20 November 1972

Editor
Ms.
370 Lexington Ave.
New York, N.Y.

Dear *Ms.*:

Since the letters you see fit to print are so flagrantly and one-sidedly selective ("self-serving" is, I believe, the expression), I doubt this will find its way into those columns; we shall see. In any case, during your own innermost and private (and, needless to say, *unpublished*) quest for *the truth*, libbywise, you might consider the following suggestion: namely, that it is naïve in the extreme for women to expect to be regarded as equals by men (despite all lip service to the contrary) so long as they persist in a subhuman (*i.e.*, animallike) behavior during sexual intercourse. I'm referring, as you doubtless know, to the outlandish *panting, gasping, moaning, sobbing, writhing, scratching, biting, screaming* conniptions, and the seemingly invariable *"Oh, my god . . . oh, my god . . . oh, my god"* all so predictably integral to the pre-, post-, *and* orgasmic stages of intercourse. Surely you're aware that such *extremes* of "expression" cannot fail to produce an ultimate and profound sense of alienation in the partner, and/or witness, to same.

I would further suggest to you that until women are able to exercise a modicum of self-control and restraint, and to maintain a semblance of *human dignity* during orgasm (clitoral, deep-vaginal, multiple, or whatever), they shall *never* gain from men the sort of respect they desire (again, the abundance of lip service to the contrary notwithstanding). Can you *seriously* imagine a man placing his confidence, his vote, or indeed any measure of real responsibility in the hands of someone he has just seen or heard (or *felt*) engaged in a *nail-digging, teeth-grinding, eyes-rolling, toes-curling, half-fainting* demonstration more suited to the kennel, or *lair,* than to the bedroom. This is an "act of love" and, by definition, should be one of heartfelt tenderness and genuine concern. There is a considerable difference, I might add, between a *show of passion* and the *rutting of a wildcat.*

Yours sincerely,

Terry Southern

New York, N.Y.

19

"*Very nice, but not what the town fathers had in mind. . . .*"

My Blue Heaven

by Anne Beatts

September 3. Today, not without regret, I dosed the remaining field mice with chloral hydrate. I don't want Matthews poaching on my territory while I'm gone. Dr. Laurie kindly offered to drive me to the airport.

September 4. Imagine me actually talking to Professor Ernest Neuberger for nearly three hours in the lobby of the Honolulu Hilton this afternoon. He was most enlightening on how bat sonar is affected by changes in atmospheric pressure.

September 5 and 6 (a.m.). Yesterday immediately after the plane landed, we were transferred to a "chopper," which brought us across the mainland to the Marine Biological Research Center. We had no chance to pay a visit to the city of Saigon. Dr. Eliot (actually a naval commander, but he prefers to be called "Doctor") says we will find everything we need here. The other newcomer besides myself is Captain Hauser, a ballistics expert. I am the only civilian in the group. I am billeted with Lieutenant O'Malley, Dr. Eliot's lab assistant. Last night, tired from my trip, I went directly to my bunk after a quick tour of the laboratory, which seems adequately equipped. A strange noise kept me awake all night: an intermittent high-pitched whistle, accompanied by low sighs. Could it be that one of the servants is sick?

September 6 (p.m.). My first inspection of the specimens. Both are *Tursiops truncatus,* or bottle-nosed dolphins, six to eight feet long and about two hundred pounds in weight. They have a way of leaping out of the water suddenly that can be very startling. The sounds I had heard during the night came from Baby, the male specimen, who has been placed in isolation in the smaller pool in order to facilitate interspecies communication.

September 7. The noises kept up all last night. Apparently the male delphinid, Baby, is signaling his desire for the presence of the female delphinid, Elvira Madigan, now in a separate pool. The dolphins were given these names by my predecessors, a Swedish-American couple. I personally dislike attempts to humanize laboratory animals. Would it not have been simpler to call them A and B?

September 9. I have started setting up sound equipment. Whenever I approach the edge of the pool housing the male dolphin, the latter leaps out of the water, arching his body and opening his mouth so that every one of the precisely one hundred needle-sharp interlocking teeth lining his upper and lower jaws is clearly visible. A considerable amount of water is splashed out of the pool with each leap. By the end of the day my lab coat is wringing wet. Damp clothes are unhealthy even in warm climates, and I am already starting to feel a chill. Would take my temperature, but the Vietnamese servants who insisted on unpacking my things for me seem to have stolen my thermometer.

September 10, 11, 12, and 13. Noises still continue.

September 14. My lack of sleep is preventing me from operating at peak efficiency and thus severely restricting my research activities. For the good of the project, I have decided to silence the male specimen's nocturnal protests by reuniting him with the female specimen.

September 15. When let into the large pool, the male dolphin, Baby, was very energetic, bounding in huge leaps from one end to the other, ricocheting off the sides, emitting loud, raucous squawks, and nudging and bumping the female with his rostral beak.

September 16. N.B.: the male dolphin has a flattened, triangular-shaped penis, which is concealed within a slit or pouch beneath the abdomen. Swimming over the female dolphin, who turns on her side or back to receive him, he inserts it rapidly into a similar slit containing the female sex organs.

After his long separation from Elvira, Baby was not content with one such conjunction, but coupled with her repeatedly. Have installed hydrophones to pick up and transmit to my tape recorder any sound that the animals make underwater. Have found thermometer but mislaid douche bag. Temperature: normal.

September 17. Dr. Eliot has taken both animals into a separate enclosure that he and Captain Hauser use for their experiments in autodirected weaponry, or "target practice," as Captain Hauser calls it, no doubt facetiously. Only naval personnel are permitted to enter the enclosure, so I spent the day sorting slides in the lab with Lieutenant O'Malley. It seems she borrowed my douche bag.

September 20. Captain Hauser acted quite strangely tonight at mess. First he picked up my napkin and pretended to find lipstick stains on it. When I pointed out that this was impossible, since I never wear any makeup, he said that I had no sense of humor. I must admit that the joke, if any, was completely lost on me.

September 21. I spoke to the cook about buying me a bathing suit on his next trip into town for supplies. Something practical that will dry easily. In studying the two animals I am becoming convinced that the male, Baby, is the more intelligent and will respond better to my tests. I have succeeded in training him to whistle four bars of "The Anvil Chorus" on cue.

September 23. Compelled to use Elvira because Dr. Eliot requisitioned Baby for the day. He, too, appears to find Baby the superior specimen.

September 24. Lieutenant O'Malley, who is following a diet, suggested I join her in an attempt to lose weight. I told her I felt perfectly healthy at 140 pounds and asked if I could enlist her help in performing an experiment. Using a respirator, I plan to put one of the dolphins under deep anesthesia and examine its brain in order to assemble neurological data. There is still the question of which animal to choose as a subject.

September 27. When I told Dr. Eliot about the experiment, he assumed I would be using Baby. I pointed out that since Elvira was more docile, she might be easier to hold down while the anesthetic was administered. Dr. Eliot said that the choice of subject was my responsibility.

September 28. My bathing suit arrived today. A French bikini. I am positive I am the victim of a practical joke of some sort. When I protested, the cook just shrugged and said I had asked for something that dried easily. Captain Hauser is probably at the bottom of this. I am surprised that the Navy is willing to tolerate these schoolboy pranks of his. Lieutenant O'Malley says if somebody gave her a bikini she would wear it "like a shot." But then she has the gregarious temperament that goes with red hair.

September 29. Lost the female delphinid, Elvira Madigan, by anesthetic death due to failure of respiration. Proceeded with examination of the brain and dissection.

September 30. Avoided seeing Baby today, since Dr. Eliot is working with him. Continued the task of dissection, preparing and mounting slides of the cortex, etc. I didn't feel up to dinner, so I had a Hershey bar alone in my room.

October 1. A distinct change in Baby's behavior pattern. On my arrival he didn't leap out of the pool to splash water on me or utter any of the high-pitched vocalizations that are his customary greeting. He ignored my presence and swam slowly round and round in a small circle at the bottom of the pool, only raising his head occasionally to take in and expel air. I feel unreasonably depressed by his attitude. This is what comes of developing attachments to laboratory animals. Decided to skip dinner again tonight. I notice I have another gray hair.

October 2. The Filipino boy who takes care of the pools and feeds the dolphins says Baby is refusing his food. I have no appetite myself and just pick at my supper.

October 3. Baby will eat nothing, not even the raw sardines that he usually loves. His eyes, ordinarily a bright, lustrous blue, are clouded over and greenish-looking. What if he dies, too? At dinner Captain Hauser said that if I keep dieting like this I will soon be wasted away to a skeleton. "I like my women *zoftig*," he added. The nerve. Later, Dr. Eliot came over to the poolside to assure me personally that I would not be held responsible for the death of any of the specimens. He said that new animals could easily be procured. How cold and unfeeling all scientists are!

October 4. Borrowed the Waring blender and concocted a nourishing fish soup. Tomorrow I will get into the pool with Baby and try to coax him to swallow it. Tonight I tried on the bikini in front of the bathroom mirror.

October 5. The condition of the male delphinid is improving. When I arrived at the pool and took off the wrap covering my bikini, Baby greeted me strangely. Weak as he was, he rose up on his hind flukes and moved backwards away from me down the pool, meanwhile clapping his flippers together as though he was applauding, and uttering a series of sharp, piercing whistles. After that, when I got into the water with him I had no difficulty in persuading him to take the soup.

October 8. Spend some time each day in the pool with Baby. Have noticed that with increasing exposure to water, human skin becomes more sensitive to tactile stimuli.

October 11. If I don't get into the water with him during the first half-hour of my visit, Baby chases me around the edge of the pool, throwing himself upon the side, nipping at my legs, and barking raucously. He is careful not to hurt me with his teeth. He is certainly more intelligent than a dog or a horse.

October 13. I have made a few modifications to the sound system. Now every noise Baby makes triggers an electronic switch that turns on a tape recorder and feeds back a recording of my voice. So every time he speaks he will hear me speak back, even if I am not there. I couldn't think of what to record, so I finally recited Elizabeth Barrett Browning's "How do I love thee? Let me count the ways ..." into the tape recorder, simply because it is a poem that I have known by heart since the sixth grade.

October 14. I was checking the connections of the sound system when Captain Hauser stopped by the pool to ask if he could bring me anything from Hawaii. He will be flying there for a few days. I was just going to ask him for new spools for my tape recorder. The next thing I knew, Baby had jumped up and knocked Captain Hauser into the water. It may be unprofessional of me, but I felt certain satisfaction at seeing him climb out, dripping wet.

October 15. Lieutenant O'Malley left for Hawaii with Captain Hauser—to visit a sick friend there, she said—so I am alone with Baby and Dr. Eliot. At dinner I questioned Dr. Eliot about his research with Baby. He said that it involved "reconnaissance" but didn't offer to let me see the work in progress. On the other hand, he became very expansive on the subject of future cooperation between dolphins and mankind. He said that soon no naval officer would want to engage in battle without them. He said that a fast-moving dolphin might sneak up on an enemy submarine and shout something threatening into the listening gear, like "Give up and go home!" (in Russian or Chinese, of course). This eerie voice from the sea could not fail to have a detrimental effect on enemy morale.

October 17. When I tried to leave the pool today, Baby caught my bikini top in his teeth and almost pulled it off before I could get free. When he plays little pranks like this, it is hard to reconcile his little-boy qualities with the sensitive spirit I know he must possess. But Baby is no mere he-man. These last tapes are proof enough of that. The Barrett Browning sonnet seems to have stirred him to his very soul.

October 18. No doubt about it. Baby is repeating the poem after me, at a much higher pitch. Even on the first listening, I could easily pick out a distinct approximation of "How do I love thee"—"da da di da di"—in perfect rhythm with my voice. Have told no one about this.

October 19. Captain Hauser back from Hawaii today with Lieutenant O'Malley, who is very suntanned. I hinted to her that big things had been happening with Baby while she was away, but she said she didn't want to hear any more fish stories. She brought me a bottle of Lady Clairol Born Blonde

Creme Rinse, to protect my hair from discoloration by the sun, she says. Her hair looks redder than ever.

October 20. Dr. Eliot needs Baby's services, and there is nothing I can say about it. Spent the day replaying the tapes. Baby is making a genuine effort to communicate. It is up to me to respond . . . to try to teach Baby all that the human race has learned through the centuries: art, literature, the wonders of civilization, and the mysteries of the human heart as well.

October 21. Baby did not return until late this afternoon. Lieutenant O'Malley was having a small cocktail party in the mess hall, to which she had invited some of the officers from the U.S.S. *Virginia*, so I was unable to do more than walk by the pool on my way there. Baby was just lying there quietly, resting, his great silver body shining through the clear water.

October 22. No entry.

October 23. No entry.

October 24. As I write this, alone in my room, the deep purple and orange of a Pacific sunset unfolds above the silver sea. Actually, I am not alone because Lieutenant O'Malley is lying on the next bunk cleaning her false eyelashes, but it seems as though I were still alone in that beautiful underwater world which no one but Baby can share. At last I am truly his, all his. And he, I think, is mine. We have been close before, but never so close as this. At the end of the day, when we know we must part, even then I can't bear to leave him. I busy myself with unessential little tasks around the pool, until the Filipino attendant arrives with his bucket of raw fish, and Baby barks a long farewell.

October 26. I am sure that Baby feels as I do. After our session today I went right to the lab and listened to the last reel of the Barrett Browning tapes. To his final recitation of the poem, he adds a sentence of his own: "I love thee, Betsy." His pet name for me. Nobody else but my mother, and one or two of the field mice, has ever called me that.

October 27. I can't be imagining it. And even if I am, looking into Baby's eyes tells me all I want to know. Only that and the touch of a flipper, or the occasional flick of his tail as he swims by, are evidence enough of his affection. What need have I for flowers, candy, or identification bracelets?

October 29. Today I worked a washer loose from one of the hose connections leading into the pool and slipped it on my finger, while Baby looked on in unspoken agreement. The world may not know what it means, but Baby and I know.

October 30. Thinking of home today. How I wish I were stepping off the train, with Baby in a glass tank at my side and a warm welcome waiting at 110 Elm Street! I know the idea might take some getting used to, especially for mother, but once she realized what a good husband Baby would make, she'd learn to accept him for what he was.

November 1. I find Baby's delphinese pronunciation more difficult to understand in person than on tape. Still, there is nothing more deeply satisfying than to hear him, at moments of great passion, tenderly repeating my name over and over in his high-pitched, quacking whistle.

November 3. I must look up some modern poets if our relationship is to progress.

November 7. Baby is working with Dr. Eliot. Decided to give myself a lift by trying the Born Blonde Creme Rinse that Lieutenant O'Malley gave me.

November 8. He liked my hair!

November 11. A sea widow again. I know I should catch up on my lab reports, but I just don't feel in the mood. I spent the day leafing through some of the movie magazines Lieutenant O'Malley's sister sends her. While she was out I practiced trying on her false eyelashes. I wonder if they would stay on underwater.

November 12. Baby still working with Dr. Eliot. I must learn not to be too resentful of the demands of his job. Nevertheless, I wonder what he finds to do all day that's so fascinating.

November 13. Our first fight. I said I didn't like hanging around all day, doing my nails and wondering when he was going to get back. He just ignored me. I suppose he'd rather I kept busy doing something useful, like dusting off the microscope slides.

November 15. Baby very restless and aggressive today, sneaking up behind me and bumping me with his beak. I told him I had a headache and went home early. I wonder if he cares for me at all. Sometimes I feel he's just using me.

November 16. Today Baby was very passionate for a change. But afterward, when I wanted to talk about Us, I could tell he was thinking of something else. Elvira, perhaps. I wonder if he is ready for another serious relationship so soon?

November 18. If only Baby would open up to me. I'm afraid he feels I'm rushing him. I know he needs time to find himself.

November 22. Another squabble today. No wonder we are bickering. The strain of this furtive, clandestine existence is beginning to tell on both of us. We can't go on meeting like this.

November 25. Thanksgiving. I wanted to share the meaning of this great American holiday with Baby, so I sneaked him some turkey that I had hidden in my napkin. He left most of it, but then his spirits are low these days. If we could only have celebrated the holiday together in our own home, things might have been different. I can see it now—Baby taking a little swim in the garden, which I have decorated with seashells. Meanwhile, inside the specially pressurized underwater kitchen, I am cooking up a batch of tempting goodies. Later, with the little ones tucked away for the night, I would read aloud from our coffee-table set of the Great Books of the Western World. I'd polish his skin three times a day if he wanted me to. I'd have a hot dinner waiting for him every night. There's no reason why my career would have to suffer. I could always find time to work at home.

November 26. My heart is pounding and my hand is shaking so much I can hardly write. Marilyn, Baby's new mate, arrives from Marineland in two weeks. I have not had the courage to break the news to Baby. My poor darling doesn't know that these may be the last two weeks we'll ever spend together! Where can I go? Whom shall I turn to? Now, even our few moments of stolen happiness are threatened.

November 30. Dr. Eliot has invited me to come along the next time he and Baby work together. He says it will be "a delicate business." Dr. Eliot and I will be on board ship while Captain Hauser monitors the test from shore. Apparently Dr. Eliot and Captain Hauser feel that my presence on board will encourage Baby, who will be at large in the ocean, to return to the ship. Something tells me this may be the opportunity we have been looking for.

December 1. The test is scheduled for tomorrow morning. Tonight for the first time I found out exactly what it is that Baby does. It's very dangerous work. I'm sure that's the reason he's been keeping it a secret. He knows how much I worry.

December 2. The test was postponed until tomorrow because of the bad weather. I am just as glad. When I think of Baby out there, alone in the middle of the ocean, a live torpedo lashed to his beak, heading for the practice target (a Vietnamese fishing boat), I grow cold with fear. What if the shell should explode before he succeeded in placing it? What if he couldn't get away in time? Would I have the courage to leap into the water and join him at last? I like to think so. But how brave he is! How selfless, defending his country at the risk of his own life, without even a uniform to pin a medal on. At least he will always be a hero to me!

(letter attached)

December 12, 1971

Dear Mrs. Burgess:
   It has now been definitely established that Dr. Burgess' death was caused by a freak accident in which a runaway dolphin torpedoed the base ship instead of the target. In the resultant explosion your daughter; our chief of staff, Dr. Eliot; and three crew members perished, as did the dolphin itself.

Although I was unable to locate the "field-mouse notebook" you referred to in your cable, I did find the enclosed notebook among Betsy's personal effects.

Once again, allow me to offer my deepest sympathies.

> *Sincerely,*
> *William Hauser, Capt. U.S.N.*

"Seymour! Stop shoving peanuts up the elephant's ass!"

S. GROSS

32

Two Historical Monographs

by Terry Southern

PURITAN PORN

The earliest authenticated documentation of what, by almost any community standards, would be considered pornography was perhaps that of the *Little Books* (1623–27), uncovered in 1919 by Professor Jason Lewellen and believed to have been among the belongings of the so-called Plymouth Pimps—one of the first of numerous groups of seafaring men who dealt in guns, rum, drugs, slaves, and indentured prostitution, plying their trade along the Bay Colony coast.

The work referred to—the *Little Books,* as they were called—was comprised of a series of line drawings, printed from carved wooden blocks, on rough rag paper, in a four-by-five-inch format. The "pages" were perforated—probably by an Addison double-hole thumb-punch—and held together in book form by coarse hemp twine.

Aside from the Settler, the characters figuring most prominently in the work, were the Indian and the turkey. A typical *Little Book* might begin with the representation of an Early Settler in a cornfield, completing preparation of a "corn-hole," his member exposed and in a state of erection. As he is about to enter the "corn-hole," his attention is attracted by something nearby—presumably a sound or movement—and he then sees, in an adjacent row, an Indian and a turkey writhing exaggeratedly in fervent coitus. The Indian is at first apprehensive at being discovered, but is quickly reassured by the Settler, who makes it known that he would like to join in the sexual activity, with eager gestures to this effect.[1]

[1] Early examples of *Little Books* rarely contained any dialogue for the reason that illiteracy was almost universal among the population.

After a brief period of sexual congress between the two men and the turkey (which would generally include both fellatio and anal intercourse, or "corn-holing," as it was known), the Settler would address the Indian, in one of the book's few captions, "You get squaw," whereupon they would be joined by an attractive Indian "princess" type, attired in buckskin and tassels, and voluptuously endowed. The two men and the turkey would then ravish the Indian maiden, in various positions and combinations. Primarily erotic, the *Little Books* were not without an occasional touch of humor, as, for example, when the turkey would be shown as having collapsed in exhaustion, leaving the two men and the girl to the more coventional techniques of lovemaking. It would be difficult, however, to overstress the role of the turkey in this early literature, though the reference was often oblique. It was widely acknowledged, for example, that the Settlers had frequent intercourse with the turkey, yet in the literature (other than the *Little Books*) and in the humor that has come down to us on the subject, it is usually the *Indian* who is sexually linked to the bird. And, according to Holbrook,[2] an oft-employed cajolery at the Settler's table, when turkey was being served, was on the order of "Why I bet this here bird is jest a-brimmin' with that good ol' *redskin-jissem!*"

The *Little Books* abound with reference to, and portrayals of, another practice known to have been fairly common among the Settlers, called "Gobbling the Gobbler," in which fellatio—of both an anal and genital nature—would be performed on the birds, by Settlers and Indians, cavorting in lively fashion the while.

Yet another depiction of high incidence in the *Little Books*—and, by present standards, perhaps the most unusual—was the act of combined intercourse and anal-head-congress between Puritan and turkey, a practice known as "Gobble Jamming." It was performed in both standing and prone positions, and required the bird to be situated upside down, between the legs of the Settler, its head toward the rear. The Settler would first enter the bird in the "normal" manner (*i.e.*, into the vent, or genitalia) and then, upon approaching climax, would reach behind him, seize the turkey's head (which had been heavily lubricated with bear or goose grease) and forceably thrust it, screeching wildly, up his

[2] Holbrook, Albert J., *The History of American Literature* (New York: Macmillan, 1952), pp. 437–38.

anus. In his *Memoirs*, H. A. Walton, at that time lieutenant governor of Rhode Island (1743), described the "Gobble Jamming" experience as being "quite extraordinary in its sheer sensory impact," and it should be noted that this remarkable practice continues today, among certain Americana-cult groups such as the DAR and their male counterpart, the SAR—though in somewhat more covert fashion than it did with their forebearers, to be sure.

THE DAWN OF CORN-HOLE

The late R. F. Donaldson, in his scholarly two-volume work, *Our Glorious Heritage*,[1] under the section on "The Early Settlers," describes the origin and practice of "corn-holing" as follows: ". . . whereupon the Settler would select an appropriate ear of corn, husk it, and press it vertically into the earth between the rows, which were approximately three feet apart. He would then move the ear up and down, in pistonlike fashion, pressing the earth firmly around it the while, until an opening the size and contour of the ear had been created. Such practices were usually done during or just after a 'wet spell' when the ground was soft, damp, and easily workable. If not, it was necessary to moisten it through the use of some liquid—water (or cider) from the traditional 'little brown jug' carried into the fields, spittle, urine, or the fluid of another fruit or vegetable, such as the tomato. When an opening, or 'hole,' of suitable measure and sufficient moisture had been completed, the Settler would lie himself atop it, lengthwise between the rows of corn, and would have sexual congress with the 'corn-hole.'

"Afterwards, if the experience was deemed to have been of an especially satisfactory nature, he might save the ear for future use; otherwise, he would simply take it back to the house at the end of the day and add it to the larder for that evening's fare.

"A settler coming in from the fields carrying a single ear of corn and with, perhaps, the front of his garments muddied

[1] Donaldson, *Our Glorious Heritage* (Boston: Little, Brown Co., 1874), vol. 2, pp. 413–14.

was immediately recognized for 'what he'd been up to,' and such situations were frequently the subject of early American humor, much of it in a ribald vein. Similarly, if the 'corn-hole' itself were discovered, the Settler was apt to be on the receiving end of some good-natured cajolery, as in the following cited by Col. Howard J. Parker: 'Stepped in yer "corn-hole," Tom, 'twernt no bigger than a cricket-nest!' or again, 'Seth Tyler has got so many "corn-holes" in his south forty, the field looks like a old rusted-out sieve!' "[2]

The transformation of the term's usuage—to mean anal intercourse—occurred during the early phase of the Revolutionary War, in the penal colonies and prison stockades which sprang up at that time. Another expression describing sodomistic practices—"up the old dirt road"—also evolved during this period, obviously derived from "corn-hole" or, more precisely, from a firsthand knowledge of its circumstances (i.e., the use of earth, or "dirt," in its practice).

The prevalence of the act, beginning with army and prison experiences during the American Revolution, was, by any standards (including those of the Mycenaean era), quite extraordinary; it is estimated by Delderfield and others[3] that "corn-holing" among the early settlers was, "from about 1774 onwards, *practically one hundred percent*."[4] This is all the more remarkable in view of its strict taboo with the Puritan Fathers a few years previous—though, interestingly enough, it was that very taboo which, accoring to the historian L. Philips Laing, probably accounted for "this epidemic of sodomy, sweeping across the land like a damnable plague,'[5] in over-reacting against the Puritan ethic—or, as Laing himself rather amusingly put it: "It was *backlash* all right—straight into the old *backside!*"

[2] Parker, Howard J., *The Roots of American Humor* (New York: Scribners, 1823), p. 164.

[3] Delderfield, Jason, *A Precious Past* (New York: Doubleday, 1937), pp. 67–73, 124–57, 322–46, *et passim*.

[4] *Ibid.*, p. 345.

[5] Laing, L. Philips, *United States History, 1776–1876* (New York: Random House, 1966), p. 651.

FAMOUS COMIC ARTISTS SCHOOL

BY BRUCE COCHRAN

LESSON # 79

THE FEMALE BODY

TO DRAW NASTY PICTURES, COMPLETE KNOWLEDGE OF THE FEMALE BODY IS ESSENTIAL. THE NEXT TIME YOU SEE A GIRL, TEAR OFF HER CLOTHES AND STUDY HER CLOSELY.

RIGHT

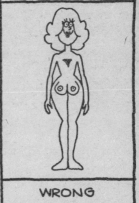

WRONG

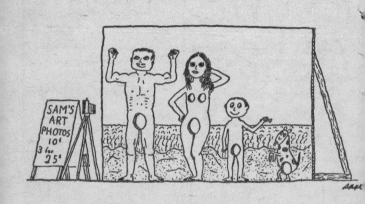

All in de Fambly

by Chris Miller and Marc Rubin

Cast of Characters

WASHY BOOKER, a typical middle-aged nigger
URETHRA, Washy's wife; an archetypal colored cleaning lady
GLOREAH, Washy's daughter; a woman of the night
MIGUEL, Washy's son-in-law; a shiftless young Puerto Rican
MR. SUBVERSKI, a Civil Liberties attorney
MR. ROSENGUILT, of the Welfare Department; a liberal

Open on WASHY *and* URETHRA, *seated behind piano.* URETHRA *plays and both sing:*

> Shootin' crap on Saturdays
> Wif de checks dat Welfare pays.
> Lord, Lord, in so many ways
> Dese are de days.

Cut to moving footage of Harlem slums, sullen men on stoops, dice games, scurrying rats, etc. Song continues:

> People call us jungle bunny,
> We jus' smile an' take dey money.
> Every year's a Cadillac,
> Now that we Negroes is Blacks.

(URETHRA: Hab mercy!)

Cut back to WASHY *and* URETHRA. *Song concludes.*

> You can't see us in de dark,
> We run de alley an' de park.
> When we want something we jus' march.
> Dese are de days.

WASHY *and* URETHRA *slap palms and grin at each other. Fade out.*

Fade up BOOKER *living room. The walls are cracked and peeling. Plaster falls occasionally from the ceiling, and garbage is strewn about the floor, partially obscuring a large zebra-skin rug. Against one wall are three color TVs, and facing them is* WASHY'S *chair, a leather massage-a-pedic special. There is also a sofa with gold lamé slipcovers and a large pillow showing scenes of the 1937 World's Fair. It is early evening.*

Enter WASHY *in tattered overcoat and raggedy shoes. With exaggerated exhaustion, he removes overcoat and hangs it in closet, revealing his leopard-skin jacket and crushed-velvet trousers. He removes a gold-brocade smoking jacket from the closet and puts it on. Wrapping an ascot around his neck, he walks to his chair, turns it on, and slumps into it. With a remote-control unit, he activates two of the TVs.*

WASHY: Urethra! Bring me mah J&B!

With great sighs of relief, WASHY *removes shoes, slips on a pair of green and purple patent-leather Hush Puppies.*

URETHRA: *(entering with a bottle of J&B):* Lord hab mercy, Washy, Ah sho' didn't hear you come froo de do'. You muss been *sneakin'* in. Uh hee hee hee hee hee hee . . .

WASHY: Ya ignorant chimpanzee, how many time Ah gotta tell ya? De only way Ah drink J&B is from a brown paper bag!

URETHRA: Mah hebbin, Ah done fo'got again. Ah'll go get it, Washy.

WASHY *(picking up* The Amsterdam News*):* Hmmm . . . what?! Urethra, lissen to dis! Dey some black folk dat been refusin' to stan' up fo' de playin' of de national anfem! Sheeit, ever' time *Ah* see de flag, chills run up an' down mah wallet.

URETHRA *(from kitchen):* Thass right, Washy: America—live off it or leave it.

Front door bursts open admitting MIGUEL, *obviously stoned, dancing the flamenco.*

MIGUEL: Jey, Washee, wha' you doin'?

WASHY *(putting down newspaper):* What Ah doin' is wait-in' fo' dat baboon ya calls a mother-in-law ta bring me mah J&B, an' den Ah gonna unlax cause Ah done had a long, hard day.

URETHRA *(entering with a bottle in a bag):* Here you is, Washy.

(Exits.)

MIGUEL: How joo can dreenk tha' sheet, Washee? Don' joo know eet rot your brain? Why don' joo try some of thees? *(Offers* WASHY *some cocaine.)*

WASHY: Get dat stuff away from me, ya garbage-head ta-male-twister.

GLOREAH *and* URETHRA *enter from the kitchen carrying hubcaps full of food on their heads.*

GLOREAH *(to the men):* Jiveassin' over. De chitlins is hot.

The BOOKERS *seat themselves about the table. There are no plates, silverware, or napkins—just the hubcaps of steaming chitterlings, fatback, collard greens, etc.* WASHY *sets his J&B before him and reaches for a ham hock.*

GLOREAH: Daddy! Momma ain' thank de Lawd yet.

WASHY: Can' de Lawd wait till after we eat?

URETHRA: De Lawd as hungry fo' our thanks as you is fo' de ham hock, Washy.

WASHY: All right, all right, le's get it over wif.

URETHRA *(standing and casting eyes heavenward):* Gawd almighty, Ah calls to ya, Lawd, fo' ya ta sactifah dis food wif yo' hebbinly power. Ah said, Ah talkin' to ya, Lawd! Ah callin' ya in de mawin', Ah callin' ya in de eebnin', Ah callin' ya in de midnight hour fo' yo' hebbinly dahgestive power.

GLOREAH and MIGUEL: Thass right!

URETHRA (*starting to bang a tambourine*): Do ya hear us, Lawd? We thanks ya fo' de ham hocks an' de greens an' fo' all dis greasy Negro food we about to eat.

GLOREAH and MIGUEL: Right on, right on!

URETHRA (*climbs on top of chair, still shaking tambourine*): Can ya dig it, Lawd? Yo' chilluns is thankin' ya fo' de chittlins, and we thankin' ya fo' de black-eyed peas, an' we thankin' ya fo' de fatback. . . .

WASHY: While ya at it, say thanks fo' de J&B.

URETHRA: . . . 'cause we gonna be *full*, Lawd.

GLOREAH and MIGUEL: Hallelujah! Work out, Momma!

URETHRA: Ah say we gonna be *full*, 'cause you is de power an' de gravy, de glory of de ham hock, de protein and de majesty an' de cholesterol, fo' evah an' evah. . . .

WASHY: Can' we get to de amen part?

URETHRA: Yeah, we gonna be *full*. FULL AT LAS', FULL AT LAS', GOOD GOD AWMIGHTY, FULL AT LAS'!

URETHRA *throws wide her arms, sending the tambourine flying across the room, and topples backward from the chair to land on the floor with a mighty thud.* WASHY *ignores her, immediately grabs a double handful of refried chicken spleens, and begins to eat.* GLOREAH *and* MIGUEL *help* URETHRA *to reattain her seat. Everyone eats, jamming food in their mouths with their hands, making loud slurping and grunting sounds.*

WASHY: Now don' nobody start askin' me no questions about what kin' of day Ah had, 'cause Ah don' feel like talkin' 'bout it.

URETHRA: Oh, did you hab a hard day at de welfare office, Washy?

WASHY: Well, now dat ya mention it, listen to dis: Ah go down to Line "C" like Ah always does, an' afta waitin' twenty minute dey tell me Ah got to go over to Line "A," an' afta waitin' anotha twenty minute dey tell me Ah was s'pose ta fill out a 91W form 'cause we's already collectin' three welfare checks a week, an' ya gotta prove hardship befo' ya can start collectin' a forf. So Ah fill out de form, an' afta waitin' *anotha* twenty minute, dey got de nerve ta tell me dat needin' ermine mud-flaps fo' de Cadillac don' qualify as no hardship. So Ah call up de lawyer from de Cibil Liverties, an' he say dat we gwine sue dey ass 'cause we can prove dat ermine mud-flaps on a Cadillac is bare necessity fo' a nigger.

URETHRA (*mouth full of food*): Hallamoofla!

WASHY: Dat's de good part. De bad part is Ah had to give 'em a list o' mah job qualifications.

GLOREAH and MIGUEL (*horrified*): Work? (URETHRA faints.)

WASHY (*throwing some J&B in* URETHRA'S *face*): Easy dere. Ah got nothin' to worry 'bout till dey's a pressin' need fo whiskey tasters, monorail motormen, or U-nited States senators.

GLOREAH: You ain' de only one who had a hard day, Daddy. Mayor Linseed done crack down on de Times Square agin. Dey raided de Hotel Baltic-Mediterranean, an' Ah had ta take on half de thirty-seventh precink ta keep mahseff out o' de Women's House o' De-tention. . . .

MIGUEL (*dismayed*): For free?

GLOREAH: . . . an' Ah swear dere ain' no worse fuck in de worl' dan a honkey po-liceman. (*To* MIGUEL) How was yo' day, baby?

MIGUEL: Oh, eet haff eets uppers an eets downers, but mos'ly downers 'cause I snort all my uppers thees morning. So I been noddin' out all afternoon.

WASHY: Miguel, it make mah blood boil to think of all dose good white folks' taxes goin' to a buncha greaseheads like yo'seff when we black folks been workin' a hunerd year to get de handouts we deserve.

GLOREAH: Miguel jus' a victim of a backgroun' of deprivation, Daddy.

WASHY: Well, den why don' he spread some deprivation aroun' an de-prive some of de folks downtown of dere TV sets an stereos an' start payin' his way 'roun' here?

MIGUEL: I tried, Washee.

WASHY: Sure. Ya done stole two aquariums fulla fish!

MIGUEL: I t'ought they were color teevees.

URETHRA: Mabdagladddbloooglb. . . .

GLOREAH: Momma, ya got ta take de food out yo' mouff firs'.

URETHRA (spits a mouthful of food on table and smiles gratefully to GLOREAH): Ah said, don' nobuddy wan' hear 'bout mah hard day?

WASHY: Whut happen? You get a cramp in yo' wriss playin' de tambourine?

GLOREAH: You go 'haid, Momma. Jus' igno' him.

URETHRA: Well, Ah been dirtyin' up de house since de sun come up. Firs' Ah spread fresh garbage all 'roun' de libbin' room. Den Ah fed de rats an' de cockroaches. Den Ah piss all 'roun' de toilet bowl an' had Miguel he'p me leave a fresh grease ring in de bafftub. Den Ah put sebbral new crack in de plaster in de bedroom an' mess up de bedsheets real good wif some of mah period blood. Den Ah wash out yesterday's toilet paper an' hunged it out de window to drah, an' den Ah . . .

URETHRA is cut off as the telephone rings. She bends down and picks up the receiver of the phone that lies at her feet.

URETHRA: Hello? (Pause.) Yeah, he here. (To WASHY) It de lawya from de Cibil Liverties Union. (Offers receiver to WASHY.)

WASHY: Ah'll git it on de ex-tension. (Bends over and picks up the receiver of the phone lying at his feet.) Uh, hello dere, Mr. Subverski. What can Ah do fo' ya?

44

Cut to Civil Liberties office. SURVERSKI *is on the phone. On his desk is an open bottle of vodka, along with other bottles labeled "fluoride." In the background, a giant panda is putting pins in a map marked "Forced Busing Routes."*

SUBVERSKI: Goot eefnink, Comrade Booker. And how are the oppressed pawns of the captialist maddog slavemasters this eefnink hmmm? *(Pauski.)* Goot! Then you vill be very interested in vhat I haff to tell you. It seems as if there might be an easier vay to qualify for the payments you so richly deserve. Have you ever considered becoming addicted to heroin? *(He removes a glassine packet of heroin from his pocket and begins toying with it.)* Because, Comrade Booker, if you vere addicted, you would merely haff to register vith the state to qualify for additional benefits to the tune of $120 a veek.

Cut back to WASHY *on the telephone.*

WASHY: A hunnerd an' twenny dollah a week? Missuh Subverski, lemme get back to ya. *(Hangs up phone and casts a sidelong glance at* MIGUEL*)* Hmmmmmmm dere . . .

URETHRA *(concerned):* Whut de lawya wan', Washy?

WASHY: He wan' me ta sign a cou't order commitin' you to a zoo! *(Turns to face his son-in-law.)* Say, uh, Miguel dere, lemme speak wif ya fo' a minute, willya?

MIGUEL: Chure, Washee.

The women go to the kitchen to dirty the dishes. WASHY *and* MIGUEL *walk to the living room.*

WASHY: Whah don' ya have a seat in *mah* chair, Miguel?

MIGUEL: Een . . . een *jor* chair?

WASHY: Sho'. Live it up, *amigo.* Ya can even turn on de vibratin' mechanism if ya wants.

MIGUEL: Oh, Washee! *(Reaches down and flips switch. Begins to jiggle visibly.)*

WASHY: Now, Miguel, ya really like dat cocaine stuff, don' ya?

MIGUEL: *S-s-sí*, Washee.

WASHY: An' reefer an' speed an' reds an' all dat other stuff?

MIGUEL: Oh, *s-s-s-sí*, Washee.

WASHY: Y'know, Ah jus' can' unnerstan' how an itelligent Hispiano-American like yo'seff can put all dat shee-it in yo' body.

MIGUEL: I s-s-suppose your J&Bees b-b-better?

WASHY: Nooooo . . . but Ah knows somethin' dat is.

MIGUEL *(suddenly interested):* Y-y-yeah, Washee?

WASHY: Yeah . . . but Ah ain' sho' Ah oughta unvulge it to ya . . .

MIGUEL: Come on, Washee, y-y-you can t-t-tell me.

WASHY: Well, de name of dis stuff is . . .

MIGUEL: Y-y-yes, Wash?

WASHY: . . . smack.

MIGUEL *slaps off the vibrator switch, launches himself from the chair, and heads for the kitchen.*

WASHY: Hey, wait a minute dere. Hol' it! Whut de matter wif ya?

MIGUEL *(turning around):* Are joo crazee? Joo know I use' to be junkie!

WASHY: Aw, one li'l shot wouldn' hurt ya.

MIGUEL: Washee, one leetle *sneef* an' I am hook again. I can't even *look* at smack. Oh, Washee, when Gloreah fin' out joo bin askin' me to take smack, she may be *muy* angry.

WASHY *(abrupt change in manner):* Well, Miguel, ya done real good.

MIGUEL: Wha' joo mean?

WASHY *(confidentially):* Ya see, Gloreah *ask* me ta check

up on ya, but Ah can see dat you clean as a whistle. Congratulations!

MIGUEL: Ohhh, *muchas gracias*, Washee.

WASHY: Well, Ah goin' out fo' a while. If Ah pass de garbage dump, Ah'll bring ya back a snack. *(Exits).*

Fade out.

Fade up on the BOOKER *living room, early the following afternoon.* MIGUEL *is sprawled out on the sofa, half passed out on drugs. He is lying on his stomach, across a pillow, so that his buttocks are lifted comically. Enter* URETHRA, *busily messing up the house, humming spirituals to herself. She lifts one of* MIGUEL's *legs and scatters some dirt under it. She exits into the bedroom. Enter* WASHY *through front door. He espies* MIGUEL *and, with exaggerated caution, tiptoes to his side, pulls a hypodermic syringe from his coat pocket, and jabs it into* MIGUEL's *rump.*

MIGUEL: ¡Jiiiiiiiiil! *(Rolls off sofa, clutching rump, staring about wildly.)*

WASHY *(rapidly replacing needle in pocket and running about the room, stamping his foot loudly):* Mah God, ya shudda seen de size of dat cockroach dat was bitin' ya. *(Stamp, stamp.)* C'mere, you. Aw, shoot, he done runned into de woodwork.

URETHRA *(bursting into room):* In de name of all God's li'l chilluns, whut goin' on out here?

WASHY: Uh, Miguel dere jus' got bit by a cockroach.

URETHRA: A cockroach? Is you O.K., Miguel?

MIGUEL: O.K.? Chure. In fac', I feel gooooooooood. *Caramba,* I no feel thees good since I stop chootin' sma—

WASHY: Uh, Ah thinks ya better lay down, Miguel. Ya can' be too careful wif dese cockroach bites, ya know. It mighta had rabies.

MIGUEL: Oh, *sí,* Washee. I jus' lie down right heeeeeeere. *(Drops back against sofa, smiling and hugging himself.)*

WASHY (*turning to* URETHRA): Now listen, ya primate, we gotta eat early dis evenin' cause dere a man comin' from de welfare office ta talk some business wif me an' Miguel, an' we don' wanna be disturbed.

URETHRA: Miguel?

WASHY: Thass right. It high time Miguel start learnin' de welfare business. He gonna have a fambly of his own to suppo't some day, ya know. An' in de meantime, Ah gonna take a nap. (*Heads for his chair.*)

URETHRA: Ya wan' me ta call ya when we ready to eat, Washy?

WASHY: No, ya missin' link, call when we's through.

WASHY *settles into his chair and picks up a copy of* Wheels & Dude *magazine opened to an ad for ermine mud-flaps, which he inspects smilingly. Fade out.*

Fade up on BOOKER *dinner table, later that evening.* WASHY *takes a last bite of watermelon and throws the rind on the floor.*

WASHY (*addressing the family*): Now Ah want ya all ta put on yo' bes' rags fo' dis social worker dat comin'. Meanwhile, Ah got ta go re-leeb mahseff.

WASHY *exits.* MIGUEL *is not looking so good; his eyes are sunken and he is holding himself with both arms.*

GLOREAH: You so' been actin' jiveass tonight, Miguel.

MIGUEL: I can' unnerstan' eet, Gloreah. Earlier I feel so gooood, an' now I start havin' the cheels.

GLOREAH: You wan' a blanket, baby?

MIGUEL: No, but could joo please to open the window? Eet's so hot in here. (*Begins to sweat.*)

GLOREAH: You sho' is actin' strange.

URETHRA: Maybe thass 'cause he got bit by a cockroach dis afternoon.

GLOREAH: A cockroach?

URETHRA: Thass right. One of God's li'l cockroaches done took a bite out yo' husbin. Hope you wasn't too spicy for his li'l stomach, Miguel.

There is a loud buzz.

GLOREAH *(talking into the intercom):* Who de jiveass ringin' our bell down dere?

VOICE FROM THE INTERCOM: It's Mr. Rosenguilt. From the welfare office.

URETHRA: Oh, mah! You better get yo' poppa from de crapper, honey.

GLOREAH *buzzes the downstairs buzzer, then walks out of the* BOOKER *apartment and down the hall to the elevator.*

GLOREAH *(banging on the elevator door):* Daddy, de welfare jiveass is here.

WASHY *(from behind the door):* Ah comin', Ah comin'.

The elevator door slides open and WASHY *walks out, buckling his pants and carrying a newspaper under his arm. There is a fresh pile of turds on the elevator floor. Cut to* BOOKER *apartment as* WASHY *and* GLOREAH *reenter.*

WASHY: Now remember, me an' Miguel don' wanna be interrupted. *(Glances at* MIGUEL, *who is still at the table, hugging his waist and gagging.)* Uh, how ya doin', Miguel?

MIGUEL: N-n-not so good, Washee. I feel kin' of seek.

WASHY: Well, dis'll only take a few minutes. Jus' sit dere an' nod.

URETHRA: Ya wan' me an' Gloreah to nod too, Washy?

WASHY: No, ya Cro-Magnon, jus' stay out de way.

WASHY *shooes* GLOREAH *and* URETHRA *into the bedroom just as there is a knock at the door. He goes to the door and opens it, revealing* MR. ROSENGUILT, *who is wearing a clothespin on his nose and trying to scrape something from the sole of one shoe.*

WASHY: Well, hello dere. You mus' be de white man from de Welfare Department.

ROSENGUILT *(blinking at* WASHY *through thick glasses):* Mr. Washington T. Booker?

WASHY: Dat's me, dat's me. Come on in, Mr., ah . . .

ROSENGUILT: Rosenguilt. Saul Rosenguilt, Mr. Booker. And where is the . . . *(Breaks off as he beholds Booker living room)* Oh, my God! Oh, you poor, poor people! Look at the filth! Look at the garbage, the squalor!

WASHY: Yeah, we sho' get lots of squalors 'roun' here, all right.

ROSENGUILT: And all because you were born with a different color skin! A biological accident! Why, Mr. Booker, do you know that Jewish scientists have studied you Negroes and found that other than your color, kinky hair, thick lips, splayed nostrils, and almost incomprehensible speech, you're exactly like us?

WASHY: Well, Ah wouldn't wanna go dat far. . . .

ROSENGUILT: But it's true, Mr. Booker. Oh, you poor people! President Lincoln may have freed you as slaves, but how could he free you from economic exploitation and cultural deprivement? And the lynchings! And the castrations!! Oh, Mr. Booker, how can I ever make it up to you?

WASHY: Well, Ah guess Ah could overlook a few of dem crustaceans if you was ta get me anotha welfare check each week. Y'now, so we can e-scape de ghetto an' mah daughter can improve her economic position in de night-care field an' mah good wife can grow her own garbage in her own garden an' Ah can have mah study of de effecks of sleep on de human brainpan.

ROSENGUILT: Oh, certainly, Mr. Booker, anything you want. . . . *(Beholds the* BOOKER *dining table): Vay iz mir!* The dining table, you said, and look at all the vile, smelly garbage you're forced to keep on top of it!

WASHY: Well, dat particular vile, smelly garbage is our dinner, Mistuh Rosenguilt. Uh, would ya care fo' a slice of watermelon rind?

ROSENGUILT: Your dinner? Well, gosh, it does look wonderful, but I'm afraid my ulcer just doesn't allow me to eat, ah, soul food.

WASHY: Think nothin' of it. *(Sweeps the contents of the tabletop to the floor with his arm.)* Jus' set yo' briefcase right down dere an' meet de heroin addick in question, mah son-in-law, Miguel.

ROSENGUILT *(extending hand politely):* How do you do, Miguel?

MIGUEL: Yurrrrrrggg! *(Throws up into* ROSENGUILT's *hand.)*

WASHY: Holy smackle! Uh, jus' go wipe off yo' hand on de sofa cushions, Mistuh Rosenguilt. We too poor to afford paper towels.

Holding out before him, ROSENGUILT *runs to sofa and wipes it repeatedly.*

WASHY *(stage whisper to* MIGUEL): Ya crazy spic, what de hell ya' doin'? Whut de matter wif you?

MIGUEL: I'm seek, Washee, sooooooo seeeeeek. . . .

WASHY: Sick?

MIGUEL: I feel like I dyin', Washee. I don' feel thees bad seence I wass weethdrawin' from heroeen.

WASHY: Wiffdrawin'? What you talkin' about? What dat mean?

MIGUEL: When joo stop chootin' the smack, joo got to weethdraw from eet, an' eet make joo seek jus' like thees . . . YURRRRRRCH!

(Throws up again, falls on floor, and begins rolling around, almost tripping the returning MR. ROSENGUILT.)

ROSENGUILT: Is something wrong with your son-in-law, Mr. Booker?

WASHY: Oh, it nothin'. Jus' a touch of de Puerto Rican flu. Don' worry, he do dis all de time.

ROSENGUILT: The Puerto Rican flu? I don't believe I've . . .

The telephone rings, cutting ROSENGUILT *off.*

WASHY: Excuse me dere, Mr. Rosenguilt, Ah be right back. (*As* ROSENGUILT *stares in stupefaction at the writhing* MIGUEL, WASHY *steps to the phone.*) Hello, Booker residence. Washy speakin'. Oh, Leroy, how ya doin'? Lissen, Ah really can' stay on de phone 'cause . . . (*Pause.*) What? Of course Ah know tonight Thursday . . . Thursday?? Oh, mah God, Leroy, Ah done totally fo'got! But lissen, Ah gotta get off de phone anyway, Ah right in de middle of . . . (*Pause.*) Ah *know* we go snipin' every Thursday night, man, but Ah jus' can' . . . (*Pause.*) Twenny-five firemen an' seventeen cop, eh? Hmmmmmmmm . . .

MIGUEL (*from across room*): ¡Ai ai ai ai ai ai ai ai!

GLOREAH *and* URETHRA (*bursting into room*): Whut de matter? Whut goin' on??

WASHY: Lissen, Leroy, Ah gotta go. Wing one fo' me. (*Hangs up, rushes back to table where* ROSENGUILT, URETHRA, *and* GLOREAH *are staring at the rolling, retching* MIGUEL.)

URETHRA: Merciple hebbins, Washy, whut de matter wif Miguel?

WASHY: Nothin', nothin'. Miguel jus' got a touch of de pickle-cell sanemia. Now you womens get back in de . . .

ROSENGUILT: Mr. Booker, you're wrong. I have wonderful news for you. This man isn't sick. He's merely going through withdrawal from heroin!

GLOREAH: Wiffdrawal from heroin?!? Miguel, you jiveass, is you wiffdrawin' from heroin?

MIGUEL: ¡Yaaaarrrrghh!

GLOREAH: You *is* wiffdrawin' from heroin!

WASHY: Oh me!

GLOREAH: Daddy, whut goin' on here?

URETHRA: Yes, Washee, whut goin' on here?

MIGUEL: *(from floor, through clenched teeth):* Yes, Washee, wha' ees goin' on here?

WASHY: Oooga booga ooga booga ooga booga . . .

ROSENGUILT: Well, I guess this means you don't qualify for another welfare payment after all, Mr. Booker, but I'm sure the example you see being set by this brave youth of Spanish origin will be an inspiration to you all during your continuing repression in the future. *(Bending to make himself heard by* MIGUEL, *who is still prone, dry-heaving weakly)* Muy bien, amigo, muy bien!

MIGUEL *throws up on* ROSENGUILT's *foot.*

ROSENGUILT *(hurriedly):* Well, I guess my work here is through. Good night, Mr. Booker, ladies. *(Exits.)*

There is an ominous silence, broken only by MIGUEL's *ragged breathing.* WASHY *looks from left to right, at* URETHRA *and* GLOREAH *regarding him stonily, arms akimbo. Abruptly, he pulls the syringe from his pocket and jabs it into his own arm.*

WASHY *(running through front door):* Hey, Mr. Rosenguilt dere, wait fo' me. Dey's another drug addick here too. Hey, wait up . . .
The door slams, cutting off WASHY's *voice.*

URETHRA: *(looking with good-natured exasperation from* GLOREAH *to the prone* MIGUEL) Oh, dat husbin of mine!

They all laugh together.

Fade out.

WOODMAN

54

O Comes to America

by Anne Beatts

It has never been established for certain why it was decided that O should go to America. O herself never knew, but then there were many things that O did not know, that she never dared to ask, just as now she did not dare to ask why she had been smuggled into the service elevator of the Hôtel Crillion or the Hôtel Hilton or the Hôtel Georges V, one of those hotels de grand luxe that Americans stay in when they come to Paris to negotiate.

Anne-Marie went with her as far as the door of the hotel room, then stopped short and waited, indicating that O should enter.

O tried the doorknob. It was unlocked. She pushed the door open timidly. There was no one in the room, which was decorated in shades of beige.

In one corner of the room was an open steamer trunk. O could see that the original lining had been ripped out so that it could be relined with dark red crushed velvet.

I do not know how long O waited before someone came out of one of the adjoining rooms. I do know that she was very thirsty.

The man who came into the room was carrying a glass of ice water.

"It must be the Hilton," O said to herself.

She was that the man was tall, with gray hair and sideburns. He looked like a military man or perhaps a member of the diplomatic corps. It was the dignity of his bearing that she noticed first. Then she saw he was wearing nothing but a transparent plastic raincoat. On his feet he wore plastic rainboots.

When he saw O, he raised the glass of ice water to his lips in an ironic toast. O could not restrain an involuntary moan.

"You will be punished for that later," he said.

The steamer trunk was quite comfortable, once O got used to the bumps and jolts as the porters carried it on board, and to the rocking motion of the ship at sea. A sliding panel in the side of the trunk allowed her to receive food during the voyage.

After the three days' crossing, they arrived in New York. O's presence in the trunk may have been explained by the fact that her passport, which was made out in a false name, listed her occupation as magician's assistant. As soon as they had cleared Customs, they went directly by private car to a brownstone in the East Sixties, a fashionable district of the city.

In another version, O arrives at Kennedy Airport. A car and a chauffeur are sent for her. She is driven to a palatial residence in Long Island. She dines alone. After dinner, she goes out into the garden, where she sees a small green light blinking at her from across the water.

On the particular afternoon with which we are concerned, O had been brought to the ground-floor lobby of a modern office building near the theater district. She was met by a woman who looked very much like Anne-Marie. The woman was wearing a black suit with a bunch of violets at the lapel. Her perfume was so strong that it completely drowned out the smell of violets and made O feel faint. She introduced O to a young man who seemed to be wearing the same scent.

When the three of them were seated in a restaurant, the young man began to talk to O very fast, in English. Although he spoke directly to O, she had the impression that his words were meant not for her but for the woman in black seated across from them, who so much resembled Anne-Marie.

He said that O was a valuable property and that they would probably agree to handle her, but only if they could be sure of having exclusive rights. He kept referring to binding contracts and ironclad clauses. O was not certain what he meant, nor to what new precepts she would be required to submit herself. The heavy scent and the rich food were making her drowsy. She agreed to whatever they asked of her. As they stood up to leave, Anne-Marie (for it was she) made a sign to O that she should accompany them.

For what seemed like an interminable time, they made O wait in an outer office, full of expensive magazines which she thumbed through idly. She was soothed by the soft splashing of the fountain in the center of the room.

From time to time young men passed by on their way into or out of the inner office. They were dressed in a curious uniform. Each one was wearing a shirt of a different color, with a tie constructed from some vivid floral-patterned material. The ties were short and very wide, so wide as to cover the entire shirt front. All of the young men were wearing two-tone shoes. Later, O would see this same uniform on a great number of the people with whom she was to come in contact.

Whenever a young man passed by the fountain, O observed that he bent to splash some of the water on the insides of his wrists and on his cheeks. The gesture had the significance of a ritual, rather like genuflection.

When O was quite sure that she was alone in the room, she went over and examined the fountain. As some droplets fell on her hand, she realized that it was not water, but eau de cologne, the same scent which was so pungent and overwhelming in the restaurant.

In the center of the fountain was a bronze plaque with an inscription. O read it quickly, nervously looking over her shoulder as if she expected someone to come in and stop her.

"This perpetual fountain of Brut cologne was provided by Fabergé, Incorporated, in grateful appreciation . . ."

Just at that moment one of the young men entered the room. He told O to go home and come back tomorrow.

On her way out, O was able to remark the name of the company: the William Morris Agency.

O returned the next day. This time she did not have to wait. She was led past the fountain to a large office. On the wall above the bare, polished surface of the desk O made out a framed portrait of two American politicians, brothers, who were both assassinated. I do not remember their names.

O was wearing the owl costume.

The man behind the desk came out and looked O over very carefully, like a butcher inspecting a carcass.

"The costume is wrong, of course," he said.

O started to protest, but fortunately the cardboard inside the mask muffled her words.

He ignored O. It was as though she existed for him only as a body or, in fact, as a piece of flesh, a lump of meat.

Could she sing? Dance? he asked.

O could not find the strength to answer.

Pressing a buzzer on his desk, he summoned one of the young men. "Get this girl some clothes," he said. "The costume bit feels right, but we could go for something more cuddly. Nobody wants to snuggle up to an owl."

Bitter tears of shame trickled down O's cheeks behind the mask.

In the week that followed, O appeared at parties dressed as a squirrel, a chipmunk, and a gerbil. No one spoke to her, but she had to endure in silence while one or two of the more venturesome tugged at her tail or tweaked her whiskers.

One day when O, dressed in her street clothes, was crossing Park Avenue or Central Park South or Washington Square Park, I am not certain which, she saw a taxi in a place where there are never any taxis. The taxi driver beckoned to her, and she got into the back seat. O noticed that the meter was not running. O leaned forward and tapped on the plastic shield with her fingertips, but all the driver would say in response to any of her questions was "What about that Lindsay?"

Suddenly, the driver turned the cab into a blind alley, stopped, and got out. O was too startled to make a sound when he opened the door on her side and forced himself upon her.

By the time O returned home on foot, it was almost dark. Anne-Marie was furious. "Where have you been? They're expecting you over at the studio."

"The taxi driver . . ." O began.

"What taxi driver? Never mind, hurry and get undressed. They're waiting."

The studio was a one-room loft in an unfamiliar part of town. Whenever O was made to go there, which was frequently, she was filmed, alone and with others, until she was so tired she could scarcely stand up. She was filmed in every possible position and from every possible angle. She was filmed kneeling, standing, sitting, from the back and from the front, with and without the blindfold. She was filmed eating spinach, taking a bath, rolling in pound cake. She lost track of the variations she was expected to perform.

In one of the best films she is seen sucking a doorknob.

As a consequence, the name O began to be mentioned in certain circles.

During this time, the man from the inner office was handling her as he had promised. O understood that although he did not own her, he owned a piece of her. Which piece, she was not entirely sure, but she knew that she must allow him to mold her to his taste (which was also the taste of a great many other people), and to make her over in the image which he considered most desirable. She was to defer to him in everything, although he was not her master. She had heard Anne-Marie speak of him as her agent.

At his urging, O entered the Miss Nude America Contest but was disqualified because of her chains.

It was at this point that O began to find out what it was like to do commercials. The squirrel, chipmunk, and gerbil costumes had long since been returned to the costumier, so O wore the owl costume. She was paid by the hour.

She posed holding a can of vaginal deodorant. The lights were overpoweringly hot. After three, four, or five hours of never-ending posing, moving, shifting her body and her hands, and opening and closing her mouth, O had slipped into a strange, trancelike state. She moved, bent, turned, twisted, and performed on cue, her body functioning, not by the force of her own will, but by another's. She felt she was no longer O, but merely those lips, those hands curving around the slim, silver cylinder—lips or hands which could and did belong to anyone. And yet she had never felt so much herself.

Her agent had once said he had "big plans" for O. O was waiting in a state of delicious terror to discover what they might be.

Her anticipation of what he might say was so great, and her terror of what she might be asked to do so strong, that when he did speak, she could hardly remember afterwards what he had said. Something about a hot property, and then "If it worked for Gloria Steinem, it could work for you . . . if we play our cards right."

O wondered who Gloria Steinem was and if she would meet her where she was going. For she would leave New York: she was certain of that.

When she arrived at the mansion, she was given a new costume to wear, one which she found strangely becoming. It was a one-piece garment, made from a shiny black satin or rayon material. The legs were cut very high in front, at such an angle as to expose the hipbones, so that the dark vee of satiny material contrasted sharply with the white flesh of her thighs. The fabric was pulled tight over O's bottom, and low-cut in back, dripping down to reveal her lower vertebrae. Her breasts were pushed up and supported by the low-cut bodice, and trembled within it like twin *flans* on a serving plate. The waist was tightly nipped in, almost but not quite so severely as to restrict her breathing. With this O wore long, black net stockings and spike heels. At her wrists were fastened white wristlets, held in place, as was her collar, by ebonite discs. O's costume was completed by the addition of long rabbit ears and a fluffy white tail.

Thus arrayed, O was informed of her new duties. She was told that she would wait upon all key holders and their guests. She would be entirely at their service while on duty. Off duty, however, she would be forbidden to see them or accept any rendezvous with any of their friends. She would wear her insignia at all times while on duty. When her services were not needed, she would repair to a restricted enclosure known as the hutch. Her official tasks would be light. Occasionally she would be summoned to the mansion, where she would be required to swim nude in the pool, pose for photographs, watch movies, and serve Pepsis. Her mouth would always remain half-open, as a sign of her complete and utter mental vacuity.

O accepted this account of her duties in perfect silence.

On the third or fourth day after the period of her service at the mansion had begun—she was not sure whether it was day or night, since all days and nights in the mansion seemed to blend together into one long bout of wanton activity, like an interminable game of strip-tac-toe; at any rate, on the fourth day, or fifth night, a white-lipped O was just completing the mandatory three hours' skinny-dipping, when an unknown man in pajamas descended the spiral staircase that led to the pool.

He leaned over the edge to reach out a hand. "You must be the new French cottontail. Welcome aboard!" he said, his pipe clenched between his teeth.

It should not be imagined that O was unhappy there. Not

at all: on the contrary; even if, once freed from its plush confines, she puzzled over the fact of its existence. Had such a mansion truly existed, or had she dreamed it into being? It gleamed in her memory like some dull opal or tourmaline, as though glimpsed through a showcase window, distorted by desire.

The mindless games, the incessant teasing, the 3:00 A.M. screenings of *The Nutty Professor*—even the ears and tail—these she had come to cherish as signs of her condition. For this reason it was both an honor and a burden when they explained that she had been chosen to be displayed, quite naked, with staples through her belly, as that month's centerfold.

They airbrushed the chains.

That left her agent no other choice than to announce their presence, on national television. The hoax was complete. There was no longer any discrepancy between O and the image that had been so painstakingly prepared for her.

She was linked to some prominent individuals.

It may have been at this time that O moved to Los Angeles. If it was not at this time, it was certainly soon afterwards. In all these months not once had O been brought before her new master, nor had his name been mentioned. But these two facts merely served to convince O that he was more powerful and terrible than any master she had known before. How could he not be, he whose devices spanned a whole continent? Here, amid the tinsel glare of used-car lots and burger palaces, of a sudden he seemed to loom larger than ever; an encounter seemed always imminent, around every corner, every loop in the freeway. To O, the very air seemed to tremble, about to spell out in sparkling letters the secret of his name.

As if to facilitate recognition, O had resumed wearing the owl costume.

She was seated in a low swivel chair between two strangers while they pried her open with questions, breaking down her defenses, penetrating her silence from all sides. A half hour earlier they had rehearsed her carefully in everything she was to do or say. "Relax, open up," they kept repeating. "Be natural." Her thighs stuck to the damp plastic seat.

Sometimes it was a man who questioned her, usually dressed in that curious uniform which had stayed in her mind since that first day she had seen it in New York. Less often it was a woman. She was expected to be, and after the sixth or eighth time she found herself, wholly pliant and responsive to their demands. I believe one of the questions used most often was "And what do you think of Los Angeles?"

Toward the end, she was completely open. Baring herself in this fashion had become completely natural to her. She could talk about the plight of the American Indian or what she had for lunch that day in front of eight million people with completely self-assured banality. Even at Roissy, when they had told her so explicitly how she would be prostituted, she had never imagined to what extent she would debase herself, or how joyously.

For it was with the shock of sudden joy that her heart almost stopped when she discovered one evening, upon returning from the studio, an envelope resting on her bureau. Inside she found an Eastern Airlines ticket to Orlando, Florida, and a sheet of paper, folded once, containing detailed instructions.

When she presented herself at the gates, there was some difficulty about the pass. Once inside, it took her several minutes to get her bearings, and she stumbled into Fantasyland by mistake. At last, sighting in a direct line from the eighteen-story spires of Cinderella's Castle, she crossed Main Street, U.S.A., skirted Liberty Square (pausing only outside the Hall of Presidents to apply fresh rouge and lipstick), and entered Tomorrowland. She was panting and out of breath by the time she found the concealed entrance to the replica of the Blue Grotto.

She felt that she was treading on sacred ground. Everything around her, everything that she had seen, was animated by the spirit of her master. She herself was merely another of his lifelike creations.

Against the far wall was a twenty-two-foot-high replica of the *Pietà*. Pressing her lips together to keep them from trembling, O touched the hidden switch. The wall swung open easily, and she stepped into the dimly lit chamber. The beads of perspiration on her forehead had already hardened to tiny balls of ice. The walls were covered with a thick frost.

O lifted her gaze slightly until she could see the casket itself. It was made from a smooth, white, marbleized substance (as was the *Pietà* outside), which had remained completely free of frost. From almost the exact center of the coffin rose a single, hollow shaft.

O took the hard black rubber mouse ears out of her handbag and fitted them to her head. Then she bent her slender neck and applied her softly parted lips to the tip of the shaft.

In a final chapter, which has been suppressed, O becomes a housewife living in Poughkeepsie, where she is visited by her former lover.

There exists a second ending to the story, in which O becomes New York's Commissioner of Consumer Affairs.

MAN
iN
TOILET
BY
Rodrigues

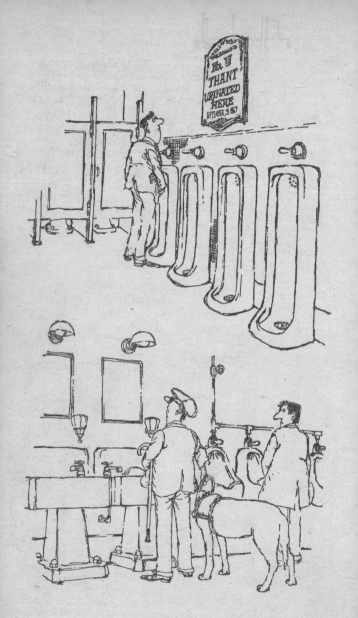

CONSTIPATED CLIENTS
MAY APPLY FOR A REFUND
AT ROOM 219-MUNICIPAL BLDG.
ASK CUSTODIAN FOR
FORM C-44:A

The I-Hate-to-Fuck Book

Anonymous

PART ONE

INTRODUCTION

How to Handle a Horny Man

Some women, it is said, like to fuck.

This book is not for them.

This book is for those of us who hate it, who have learned through hard experience that sex is the stiff fine we gals must pay for our marital misdemeanor. Others may find their mons twitching and oozing at the mere thought of an impending private, but for me . . . peter palls mound!

More times than I care to remember my husband has come home from work rubbing his gluttonous groin and exclaiming, "Golly, am I horny! How soon do we fuck?" No matter how busy *I've* been all day, he expects me to drop everything and serve up a piping hot vaginal pie for him to dig into the minute he walks through the front door.

Sometimes I get so fed up with these pubic picnics that I could send up one loud and long sperm wail! I may run the kitchen the rest of the time, but when it comes to popping the self-rising-dough stick into an unheated ovarian oven, he's the baker and I'm just another tart.

Is there no justice in conjugal court? Women are, after all, the ones who must bear the weight of intercourse: in my case, six feet and 195 pounds of ponderous-pudding plunger. We simply *lie there* while our rough-ridin' ramrods drive their longhorns down the Old Jism Trail, herd the beef into the clitoral corral, and rush off to spend their pay in the uteral saloon. Our "freedom of choice" is limited to taking it missionary or doggie style.

I suspect there isn't a married woman in the country who hasn't had one of these unnerving experiences. Hubby appears after a workout in the garden, sticks his nose in your crotch, and says, "Mmmmm, boy, that smells good. I'm so horny I could hump a horse." But before you can get to the phone and call the stable, he's mounted you!

On top of that, the men just come and go, while we gals get stuck with cleaning up the mess. It might be more tolerable if Cupid's cloister was coated with Teflon, but, sad to say, anatomical fixtures lag way behind modern culinary science when it comes to simple convenience.

Often I have lain prostrate on a sea of sheets, helpless, as his pelvic pirate forced open my hairy hatchway and plundered the gold in my little treasure box, and thinking there *must* be another way. Inter *can't* be the only course! How can the common housewife save her downy delta from erosion by a testicular torrent without damming up the fertilizing flow for good?

Talking with some lady friends at lunch one day, I discovered they were as upset as I was over being forced to play post-office box for third-class males. Our attitude was that if men were anxious to deploy their gonadal guerrilla, let them practice some hand-to-gland combat!

Then one of my friends confessed that she had recently been experimenting with alternatives to intercourse, ways to give her husband satisfaction without rending the delicate fabric of her velvety vulva. With the subject broached, the others present, yours truly included, allowed as how we, too, had oft entertained similar thoughts.

Our casual luncheon meeting thereupon turned into an idea-swapping session on ways amd means to remove a man's horns without getting gored ourselves. This guide is the result of that effort.

Here you will find five recipes, each requiring only rudimentary kitchen skills, which will sate a fellow's hunger while leaving your precious pantry full for those *special* occasions that call for an elegant opening and a lavish spread. There is also a generous dollop of household hints to help you through all manners of salacious straits quickly and with ease.

So, if you too hate to fuck, and believe that your rare and valuable organ should be played with discrimination and care—not banged like a phallic cymbal—read on! Then, next time that stout redheaded visitor pops up at your labial lobby looking for a warm and cozy womb at the Y, you'll know how to take the matter in hand and dispense with the unwanted guest.

PART TWO

RECIPES

1. **Organ Grinder.** Just as the hoary prescription of "A little hair of the dog that bit you" is valid for hung-over husbands, another axiom, "Organ meats are best for the organ," holds true for horny hubbies. It seems the soft, squishy texture of these cuts is a fair approximation of milady's passion passage, and the discriminating onanist would as soon slip it to a pound of sweetbreads as he would to the candy channel itself.

The recipe I devised (and which has become one of my husband's very favorites) calls for a half-pound of veal kidneys in the drum of the cement truck. Pack the kidneys in the drum of the cement truck (found in better toy stores everywhere), taking care they are loose enough to be penetrated and tight enough to remain in place. Your fellow can grind merrily away at his organ, cranking and rotating the little drum to suit his own taste, while your monkey takes the day off.

Unfortunately, my husband hates liver, a cavil that precludes me from preparing the popular simulation (sometimes called "Portnoy's Ploy") of slapping a piece of calf's liver around the insatiable cable and turning on the juice. For those men who *do* like liver, I pass along a recipe concocted by Dr. Christopher Miller, sex critic for one of our leading national publications. Dr. Miller suggests placing slabs of liver inside a gerbil wheel and letting the rodents have a good, long workout. Lacking gerbils, you could hook up the garden hose and make a tiny waterwheel that would be just as effective.

2. **Hot Pork Sandwich.** Next time he asks you to fix him a quick box lunch tell him the snatch shop is closed for repairs and offer instead this gonadal goody: Horizontally halve a ten-inch loaf of French bread and scoop out a trough lengthwise in each piece. Fill the twin cavities with a thick layer of

soft, smooth cream cheese and place the halves back together, securing them with rubber bands or vise clamps. Make sure there is just enough room at one end for him to enter. Now glide the lubricated loaf over his pulsing pylon and watch his face contort with ecstasy as the staff of life embraces the lively staff. He can twirl it, he can pump it, he can pound it, he can jiggle it. And when he's through, you can chuck the whole shebang into the garbage pail. No mess, no fuss, and pussy is left undisturbed.

3. Creamed Potatoes. Some guys just aren't satisfied unless they have something approaching human size and shape in which to burrow their tumescent tuber. You can solve this problem by simply removing the pedestal from a solid (not wire) dress designer's dummy (leaving a just-right hole in the base) and filling the bottom half with warm mashed potatoes. About five pounds should do the trick. You could even remove the pinkie tips from a pair of old rubber gloves and glue them to the breasts for counterfeit nipples. Now, place the whole production on a vibrating bed (or in the back seat of a car traveling over rough roads) and watch him dig those spuds!

4. Molded Mons Salad. If it's venerealism you're after, try this testicle treat: Obtain a plastic working model of the female reproductive system from a supplier of medical-school instructional aids, cut it in half lengthwise, and fill each half with ground-up raw haddock mixed with mayonnaise and softened butter. When the mixture has set, remove it from the molds and fix together with a layer of Liederkranz cheese. Voilà, pseudo pubes! What with the simulated shape, cushy feel, and pungent odor of raw fish and cheese, you'll have him believing he's mining a twenty-one-carat gold piece.

5. Tabby's Delight. Should your swain tire of food fucking and decode to put dicky on a diet, you can still glut his groin using nonvegetable matter. There's a marvelous product on the market that all countercoitalists should know about. It's called Petromalt, and it's sold at pet stores as a cure for the feline condition know as "hair balls."

To give your spasm chasm a well-deserved breather, apply a generous coating of the stuff to his preening private, garnish with bits of Purina Cat Chow, and give Tabitha her head. When that sandpaper tongue works its way up to his tender, tantalized tip, you'll see the biggest gol-durn eruption since Vesuvius came all over Herculaneum and Pompeii.

PART THREE

HOUSEHOLD HINTS

1. Those ghastly diaphanous nighties, crotchless panties, and fishnet-mesh rompers that he orders from Frederick's of Hollywood are perfect for straining jams or applying wood stain and varnish to unfinished furniture.

2. His sexual urge will be much less pronounced next day if you take care to step his dormant kielbasa in kerosene overnight.

3. You liberated ladies can put those discarded bras to excellent use in your gardening. Tacked to a wooden frame, the distended cups make for a cozy place to start tomato seeds come spring. Or, put them over tender young seedlings, when a late frost threatens.

4. Should you be having breakfast in bed together, and he slyly hints that "something's just come up," a cup of scalding hot tea or coffee down the front of his pajama bottoms should take the starch out right quick.

5. I guarantee that he'll be much less insistent in nocturnal submissions if you tape the latest national statistic on venereal disease to the inside of the medicine-cabinet door. Add to his nighttime reading a vivid, scientific description of the effect gonorrhea has on the male sex organ, and he'll be sure to pass up your vaginal stew for fear of getting VD dinner instead.

6. The love creams, passion jellies, and orgy butters he places so conspicously on your vanity with monotonous regularity are just dandy for keeping your garden tools in tiptop condition.

7. Is he the type of rugged chap who demands proper sound effects from you while converting your precious posy into a Venus open-fly trap? If so, Scotch tape several of your recent grocery bills to the bedroom ceiling, and you will have no difficulty at all in exclaiming, "Oh! Oh! my God, my God . . ."

S. GROSS

Pruzy's Pot

by Theodore Sturgeon

Dear Fred:

To come right to the point, do you think you could find us a house in your part of the world?

I know this comes as a surprise to you. Well, hell, this letter is probably a surprise, knowing me and how I don't write letters. Really sorry about that. Ever since I married Niwa two years ago we've been so busy that there just hasn't been time, and besides, I hardly ever wrote anyway, even before. But I know you've heard something about what we've been doing, if you've read anything I've published recently. In case you haven't, I'll give it to you briefly: we're trying to work out a survival life-style in this crazy, crowded, complicated world we live in. Nothing theatrical; Niwa and I are both deadly sick and tired of sitting around with bright-eyed malcontents, all knowledge and no experience, complaining about pollution and corruption in the body, mind, and soul of man. It hit us all of a sudden, one night after one of these mouth-marathons, that anyone who has a complaint ought to have to qualify to be certified first. I mean, here's somebody who thinks it's just awful about the dirty water and the foul air. What is he doing about the solid waste he creates in his own house? What kind of poison factory is he driving, and does he keep it running in such a way as to minimize the junk it puts into the air? Does he support government people he knows are corrupt, or by apathy just let them go on corrupting? The more we heard this kind of crap from these hobby-gripers, the more we felt that a man should qualify to drive a bus or cut an appendix or run a ferryboat. Or vote. And if we were going to be honest about it, we had to look at ourselves. Point a finger at anybody and you'll find you have three fingers pointing at you.

Sorry, Fred—I didn't mean to preach, but you've got to have this background. Once we faced these things we decided to get out of the plastic cave we were living in, with the chrome kitchen and all the little bells and buzzers that told us when to take the defrosted food out of the automatic oven and when the heavy phosphates were flushed out of the polyester double-knits, and headed for the hills to plant some honesty and see if we could harvest some survival. And you'll never guess where we found what we were looking for: in the "Houses to Rent" in the Sunday paper, the first one we checked out. And yet it wasn't all that simple, because when we got there to look at the place (2-bdrm, frplc, sec, Ch & pets OK) there were cars all over the mountainside and the agent was running guided tours through the house every seven minutes. Secluded two-bedroom houses with fireplaces are not all that common so close to downtown. It was everything it claimed to be and rent was most reasonable. It was also funky and creaky, with some interior wallboard smashed and cracked, a few broken windows, the most jarring paint job inside I have ever seen (did you know there are seventeen Day-Glo colors? It had them all), and no more than about eight pounds' water pressure. However, it did have more than a half-acre of ground, and being on a knoll with the wild part of a park just across a narrow road, it was absolutely private.

Niwa, being Niwa, full of enthusiasm and articulateness, spouted and jetted all our ideas about survival techniques in the late twentieth century, man versus plastic and the organ versus technology, and the whole rap, interspersed with enthusiastic "What a great corner for the rabbit hutch" and "Here we dry sassafras" kind of things. You haven't met her yet, so I have to tell you that she lights up the landscape even when she isn't enthusiastic. When she is—wear your welding hood. The agent, a faceless type with a clipboard, took notes and said, "Don't call us, we'll call you," and we left to look up more houses.

But that night we got a call from the landlord. He talked to Niwa and he talked to me. He had a deep voice that sounded something like that monotone you get from someone who's had a laryngectomy and uses stomach wind—a sort of controlled burp—but not exactly that either. He said very little about himself except that he was in some kind of biochemical research and he owned a couple dozen properties around. We didn't care about that part of it just then; what mattered was he said we could have the house if we wanted it, and we wanted it. He sent over a lease by messenger and we paid two months and that was that. The lease was standard except it said we were to let him put in another half-bath. It spelled out that we could do anything we wanted with the house and grounds except mess with the plumbing. I never heard of a landlord like that and I never saw one either, not even this one, because he died a few months later.

I wish I could remember that conversation in detail or had taped it or something. It would have explained everything. Or almost. Maybe I didn't listen too carefully because mostly it was Niwa in the electric explosive ways of hers expounding our theories of survival; how to use tansy (which when growing repels ants) and toads for insecticides instead of chemical sprays, and how barter (two loaves of sourdough for a brake job on the VW) is better than money, and how much better it is to live without clothes, design them yourself and have something money couldn't buy. The thing was, this landlord, who said his name was Jones although we found out later it wasn't, he liked everything she said and that's why we got the house.

So we really put roots down—in several senses—and dug in. It was kind of great, Fred. Anybody who tells you that working out this kind of life-style is easy, or that there's an easy way to do it, is out of his gourd. The same thing is true of anyone who implies it's cheap. And you make mistakes. When we imported a thousand ladybugs to help the toads fight insects in the garden, what we got was a lot of fat toads. We also discovered the mysterious communication network that exists in the netherworlds. Like, nothing is more specialized than a hornworm, a beautiful animal that grows very large and is so perfectly adapted to tomato plants that you can stand with your nose seven inches away from one (and *it* is seven inches long) and not see it, while it is stripping the plant of leaf, bud, flower, and fruit. Now: who sent for the son of a bitch? Likewise gophers. Nothing had grown on that little quarter-acre for years but Dichondra. All of a sudden gophers are all over, tearing up the beets and carrots and going down the lines of butter lettuce like a wire contacting phone poles. Who sent for *them*? Then, of course, there was Sonya—she's the more-or-less dog we have—who in a flash could pursue a gopher clear across the garden . . . diagonally . . . eighteen inches deep all the way. Which meant fencing.

All the same there's the way brussels sprouts grow, which has to be seen to be believed, and baby ears of corn eaten raw, and vine-ripened tomatoes, like nothing else you ever flang a fang into, and chard, and carrots tenderer than a titman's dream of the ultimate nipple ... and then the barter that went on, and a kind of understanding of where it's all really at that comes to you only if you can get naked and work soil with the sun on your back and the wind blowing through you rather than on you, and you plant a seed and, lo, it comes up, and it forms and buds and flowers and makes, and what it makes you eat—you eat it into your same body that did all this, no cellophane, no supermarket, no middleman, no tax. No, it isn't easy; no, it isn't cheap. It is, however, in these declining years of twentieth century, one of the few realities that is not a bummer.

But there I go. What I am writing to you about is can you find me a place, and especially now after all that I have to tell you why. It's the toilet, the new toilet.

I think I already said it was the lease. That was pretty weird by itself; there are plenty of things that house needs, and there's nothing wrong with the facilities that are already there. But you don't complain when a landlord wants to improve your place, even when he insists on it. So sure enough, after we'd been there ten days or so, here comes a truck with the agent and two guys, one a deaf-mute five feet across and the other one the skinniest man I have ever seen. Nobody said much, and we were busy outside most of the time. They converted one of the two big walk-in closets in the big bedroom into a nice little toidey with a sink and a pot and fluorescent lights and not-bad wallpaper and wall-to-wall carpet on the floor. There was a door from the bedroom and one from the hall—that was the new one.

And there was the pot. The agent had nothing to say about it—I don't think he knew anything—except that Mr. Jones had supplied it, that this and no other was the one he and his lease had specified, that it was a brand-new design, and that in the remote eventuality we didn't want to use it, we didn't have to—there was always the old one; and we had to admit that the old one was adequate.

That happened to be the day Pruzy Penntifer arrived from New Zealand. I've told you about her, haven't I? Used to be Niwa's roomate in London before we were married. Niwa made a special friend of Pruzy because she never could figure her out. She was the English-speaking-world's number-one straight, a noncussing virgin, "impermeable, impenetrable, and insurmountable," as someone once said, so guarded against men that the armor was up against women, too, in case one of them be used by some man to infiltrate. To Niwa, who has always been interested in the matter of being honestly alive, Pruzy was a fascination and a challenge. Anyway, she was on a world trip and was to stay with us for a week, and Niwa had been spitting on her hands in anticipation for a long time. Pruzy had been warned in advance about our life-style and that we aren't about to change it for anybody, although the last thing we'd ever do is to persuade anyone else to adopt it. "I'll live by your rules in your house," Niwa would say, "and you can live by your rules in my house. But when you expect me to live by *your* rules in *my* house, you go too damn far." So we didn't get a real look at the toilet until after it was installed, because we had to go to the airport for Pruzy while the men were finishing up; they were gone before we got back, everything cleaned up and the key under the mat.

Pruzy you wouldn't believe—tall and slender and dressed in blacks and browns. The one word for her is "contained." Her chain-mail clothes contain her, and you get the idea her skin contains her body the same neat way. She has one of those self-contained mouths that has never sucked on anything but itself and does a lot of that, and eyes coated with one-way glass. She talks funny, but not funny like like most Australians, who to the American ear put a fine Bow-bells breadth to the simplest words; her laminated gentility contains even that.

We gave her the guided tour of the house and garden, winding up in the big bedroom, which was to be hers while she stayed. The small one was my studio, and we'd sleep in the living room, which was fine with us—we mostly did anyhow. This way we could come and go without bothering her, if that's what she might want. And of course she had her own sink and pot, the latter of which made a fine ending and climax to the tour. The big closet in the northwest corner was gone, and there was a new high-up half-encasement in the outside wall, a built-in medicine chest, a very nice little washstand with a hemispherical imitation-marble bowl and gold colored fittings, and the ... the ... well, the pot.

It was wider and lower than most, bulbous. It seemed at first to have scales, tiny close-set ones, but if you closed your eyes and touched it, it was perfectly smooth. The seat was covered and there seemed to be no way to lift the cover—and indeed there was not; it took a little fumbling to discover that the raised pale spot on one side was a control. It must have (I thought at the time) some sort of electrostatic system, like those elevator buttons you don't depress but just touch, because on contact the cover slid back like an eyelid, exposing the bowl. I got only the one glimpse of a complicated contour inside, obviously moist (though I saw no standing water) and deep red. And then, only half meaning to, I hit the spot again and the cover slid silently shut, whereupon the whole thing went (with overtones of joy and controlled power) softly *hroom, hroom, hroom* ... like the revving of a distant muffled motorcycle or a tiger's purring.

I heard a tiger purr once.

Just as I wish I could recall that one phone conversation with the late Mr. Jones, I wish I had been watching Niwa's face and especially Pruzy's, but I was preoccupied with my own reactions. There was something profoundly unsettling about that piece of plumbing. I had a crazy artist friend once who painted the inside of his toilet with high-gloss enamels, bright red and cerise and ivory, so that when you opened it up it looked like a huge slavering mouth with a wet tongue and sharp teeth. That was unsettling, too, but it was also funny. This one wasn't funny. For one thing, the shock value of my friend's work of art lay in the fact that in all respects his was a conventional fixture, with his efforts applied to it, whereas this thing was all of a piece—eerie all over. I think Niwa expressed it best when we talked about it later, after Pruzy had gone to bed. She said, "I think if it looked as if it might bite, I could laugh it off. But it doesn't. It looks as if it was going to *smile!*"

We lay quietly for a long time, thinking about sitting down on that smile. Then one or the other of us—it doesn't matter which, because we both felt the same way—said, "Well, she can have the damn thing." And we left it at that.

During the night I heard it going *hroom, hroom,* twice.

The next day we got up and went to work as usual, me in my studio and Niwa in the kitchen and garden. Pruzy slept late, getting her time zones sorted out, and when she emerged and encountered us naked, the way we always are in the house and yard, she took it imperturbably—well, she'd been told, she knew what to expect, and besides, nothing—*nothing*—can crack that chick's unassailable front. She, of course, stayed not only dressed, but groomed.

It must have been three days later that we began to notice how much time Pruzy was spending in her nonbath bathroom. She always shot the bolts on both doors when she went in and unlocked them when she left—a purposeless ritual, but then so is nineteen-twentieths of all ritual privacy. (An airline hostess once told me a little old lady borrowed a safety pin from her and she found it later in the tiny ten-inch curtains over the porthole in the john, where Granny had pinned them closed—at seven hundred miles per hour and thirty thousand feet—to guard against Peeping Toms.) Niwa and I had no need or desire to go in there, so she might just as well have kept the outside door permanently locked, but once she'd established the ritual she kept it up, that being the nature of ritual. So we always heard the bolts, and though we had no wish to pry, we couldn't help but notice she was spending an awful lot of time in there.

"Maybe she likes to read there. Lots of people—"

"Pruzy is not a reader," Niwa said positively. "She really thinks she knows everything she needs to know." Which figured. People like that have achieved a kind of balance, and they'll fight like hell to keep it. One of the best ways to do that is to put the brains in suspended animation.

It took about five days for us—Niwa, really—to realize she wasn't using any toilet paper. That became an increasing fascination, too, as the days went by. And they went by, too: Pruzy postponed her departure for a week and then for another, and started to chip in to the exchequer before we could suggest it ... and she was no trouble, really. But we did wonder about the toilet paper. It wasn't anything you could come out and ask, either. Not with Pruzy. She was company of a sort for Niwa when I'd go through my marathon writing sessions, or my marathon hell-alone sessions, and she helped efficiently with the house ... and got to where she was spending three hours a day in her john.

She went into town one day and got her visa extended. Then there was a phone call when she was out, about a naturalization form. "I think," Niwa whispered to me one night, "she's going to immigrate, take the vows, join the melting pot."

"No pot in the world could melt that one," I remember saying. I was wrong.

Sonya had puppies. She would do that from time to time, concealing her intentions until it happened, then suddenly not being there at chowtime. Then it was a matter of beating the bush and crawling through dark crannies until you found out where she'd spawned them. If you couldn't, the pups would give themselves away sooner or later, mewling and yapping. They were usually a sorry lot. This time was no exception. She'd found a crawl space under the house and had her puppies way underneath. I bellied under some forty feet before I found them, and it happened to be right under Pruzy's bathroom. Though puppies were my immediate preoccupation, I couldn't help noticing the plumbing. There were hot and cold pipes to the washstand and a cold feed to the toilet, shiny new pipe. And you know what else?

Nothing else. No waste pipe. I mean, no sewer, no outlet. I'm telling you, Fred, nothing. And don't tell me I could be wrong. Water pipes are half-inch, maybe three-quarters, but waste plumbing is big, man—four to seven inches.

I didn't say anything to Niwa about it, but the next day I went up on the roof. There was a vent pipe, sure enough. I hung an ear on it. Air was passing through it all right—*inward*. Before I could check it out, it stopped, and then started again.

Outward.

Fred, it was going in and out about twenty-five to the minute. Like breathing.

I didn't say anything about that to Niwa either. Not then.

It was the next day—yesterday—when the girls were out that I decided on a confrontation with the thing. Well, to tell the truth, it was my lower gut that decided me. I was on my way to the old familiar comfortable john when I suddenly thought of that purring pot of Pruzy's. (In our minds it has become completely hers, neither of us ever use it.) So in I went.

There it sat, low, wide ... waiting. I reached down and touched the pale hump, and cover snicked back instantly and almost silently. I looked down into that moist, convoluted red surface and worried a little. Well, I thought, O.K., but one at a time, all right?

So, man-style, I stood in front of the thing and let fly.

Fred, the best possible way to describe what happened is to say it gasped in astonishment. I don't think it had ever met a man before. For a split second a black orifice appeared way down deep, then the sidewalls sort of bulged and rubbed together and it, well, swallowed. Well, dammit, you don't have to believe me. But now that I'm started I'm going to tell it all.

I'm not usually a stubborn guy, but I'd come in there to do something and I meant to do it. Also to find out something. So I sat down to finish what I had started.

For a moment that thing and I, both of us, I'll swear, we held our breaths. Then I had a rush of brains to the head and grabbed the family jewels and held 'em up as high as I could. I mean I wanted answers, but I wasn't about to walk out of there singing soprano, and it dimly occurred to me that this thing might be designed to remove anything it hadn't programmed itself for.

Well, there was this tense moment, like the one in the cowboy pictures when the walkdown is over and the shooting hasn't started yet, and then I let fly. I submit to you that I'm not characteristically one of those strain-and-ponder types who has forty-minute ritual. I don't go till I have to, and when I have to, I go altogether.

I never fazed this thing. At the first show of anything, something warm and moist zocked me gently and firmly on the bull's-eye and—now, dammit, I can see your face as you read this, Fred; it's *true*, also it's not funny—and it applied just as much suction as I supplied pressure. It made the whole thing so easy and so fast that even before my reflexes could pucker me up I was done. I came up off that thing as if it was hot—which it wasn't—and even in that split second I was aware of why Pruzy never had to use toilet paper. I suppose I made a deal of noise, too. Next thing I was aware of I was flat on my face in the hall. You want to escape as fast as I wanted to escape, you pull up your pants first. And behind me the damn thing's going *hroom, hroom, hroom,* happy as catnip.

Well, that's the story, except for Pruzy. I guess I was a little hysterical when the girls got home because I was yelling that we had to move; I mean, flat out, no argument, we were getting out of here. As soon as Pruzy got the gist of it she came alive like I have never seen before. Could she have the place? Could she take over the lease? And Niwa, flabbergasted, shouting at me what do you mean, move? Are you out of your thing, man? What about the garden?

The picture that overrides that whole wild scene is the imperturbable Pruzy, eyes glowing, voice breathy saying over and over, "Please, you must, you know. I love this house. I love it, love it, love it. . . ." The only way I could cut the chaos was to take Niwa out in the car then and there and tell her what happened.

She took it hard—not the idea of moving; you can always get another house. Not even the garden, though it's a shame after all that love and work, because you see, once you clear ground and plant something, that's more important than harvesttime, you take so much away with you. Why Niwa cries a lot is that she feels she's failed. She'd thought she would go to any lengths, do anything, live any way that would bring us closer to the cycle of earth and natural food, recycle, replenish ... but she had to draw the line at Pruzy's pot, which (like all of us) lived off the products of other life-forms. If it was bred to deliver special joys, that was no different from the function of fragrant flowers or bright sweet fruit, right? But she couldn't cut it, and that made her whole conviction about life-style look like a hypocrisy and a failure, and she cries a lot. For all that, neither of us can take the image of Niwa, too, coming out of a two-hour session with Pruzy's pot, saying breathily, "I love it, love it. . . ." Ecch.

So find us a house, Fred, as far away from here as you can, and if it's one with plastic walls and monofilament rugs and a kitchen full of dials and bells—fine, man, fine.

Wiffers and Cooties and Lungers on Strings

These are a few of my favorite things

by Doug Kenney

CHAPTER 1

"You can pick your friends, and you can pick your nose, but you can't pick your friend's nose."—Benjamin Franklin.

What is wrong with this picture? You are waiting in a Greyhound terminal and observe an aged gentleman, bracketed by worn shopping bags, reading a *National Enquirer*, and quietly mining for nose gold. You know, picking a winner. Striking pay dirt, he disappears with the swag behind his paper and reemerges a moment later, pages rustling guiltily and his snaky little eyes darting every which way.

Careful now, don't be fooled. Despite the front-page pix of two-headed starlets and freeze-dried toddlers, the *real* headline reads OLD GREEK IN BUS STATION EATS OWN BOOGERS AND LIVES!

Shocking, you say? You mean some people actually . . . ? The words stick in the throat. Well, so would that yummy rope of butterscotch if he didn't rewind occasionally, so have some compassion. (Bronchitis, America's number-one appetite crippler!)

Just stop at any traffic light, watch the guy alongside, and you may be surprised, certainly nauseated, by the rampant ambergris poaching on our nation's highways.

Yes, mucus recycling—once thought to be the exclusive province of tots and dotards—is enjoying new interest among sensual adventurers. Bored with hand-held oscillators, rubber torsos, and clever chimps, today's jaded thrill-seekers often feel that they have "lost touch" with themselves and yearn to return to their roots. Tiring of that, it is a small step to sexual reversions such as loogie-hoarding.

Symptoms appear early, often as a marked fondness for rolling up and saving those little balls of rubber cement. But with practice, this childhood pasttime may blossom into such elaborate reversions as the Incredible Sticking Booger. Simply, the nose nugget is rolled around on the fingers until the proper consistency is obtained. Then, it is passed from finger to finger, from hand to hand, and from hand to ... other areas. Distinctly personal styles soon evolve, ranging from a rigid formalism reminiscent of Japanese tea ceremonies to inspired improvisations recalling the ball-handling of Meadowlark Johnson.[1] Calorie counting? Then play *bombe plastique*. Stick it anywhere! Under a theater seat, on a taxi door handle, between a firm handshake (don't be timid—he just planted one on your coffee spoon.)

Disgusted? So were the reactionary bluenoses who banned Joyce's *Ulysses* and hounded Thomas Edison into an early grave. Be bold, explorer, and rediscover the pleasure garden growing right under (or, as with our elderly friend, above in) your nose. Any quiet grotto or untraveled nook can be a gold mine of exotic delight. Take your search inward toward those marshy undergrowths where a treasure trove of yeasty and intriguing foreign matter awaits. Mine workers of the world, unite! You have nothing to lose but your lunch.

CHAPTER 2

"In the permissive atmosphere of the '60s, the news media were avid chroniclers (and, some believe, instigators) of the much-heralded 'sexual revolution.' Any Tom, Dick, or Abbie with a mouthful of obscenities and a headful of LSD was practically guaranteed a nightly audience of twenty million viewers on evening network news.

[1] *The Guinness Book of World Records* gives the nod for jam-juggling over time to Scotty Peterson, eleven, of Orlando, Florida. Peterson kept it in play for 117 hours, 37 minutes, excluding naptime.

"Many Americans now hold Mario Savio's Berkeley-based 'Free Speech' movement as primarily responsible for later public acceptance of such porno flicks as Deep Throat *and* Behind the Green Door. *'These campus messiahs of the "Free Smut" philosophy,' Billy Graham recently stated on Barbara Walters' Not For Women Only television program, 'have led millions of impressionable young people into a moral cesspool. Sometimes it gets me so angry I have to stalk the park and suck off a seeing-eye dog just to shake the jitters.'"*
—Time *Essay. "Where Have All the Flower Children Gone?"* Oct. 38, 1973.

I can't exactly explain why I wrote that. This article is supposedly only about Fun with Mung, but until I run through this Jamaican I received in quantities under one ounce from my good buddy Jon Jones, it may tend to . . . wander a little.

Also, the tube just reported that they ruled *Behind the Green Door* obscene. Jesus, I saw it and they weren't kidding, it really *is*. Don't get me wrong, though. I personally would eat out Marilyn Chambers after eight laps around the track on a muggy day. Nine maybe. And as obscenely as possible—rrrrrraaaaawwwwrrr you eat so good oh baby oh God *you eat so good gimme eat God please gimme gimme.*

Oops. Tony Hendra said this was supposed to be under two thousand words . . . probably afraid that if I had enough space I'd blow the whistle on the Atomic Mole People. *Yes . . . strange visitors from another zip code and who, disguised as perfectly harmless fire hydrants, are secretly plotting to turn us into human Roto-rooters and slaves and living toilets and*

The headaches again. Please . . . no more, please . . . yes, I'll stop *I said I'll stop*

There. Better now. Physical pain . . . how well they know our individual weaknesses.

Leaving the nose for just a moment (just pausing long enough to remind listeners that nose *polish* does wonders for doll furniture), let's drop in on the wide world of coprophilia. Coprophilia, as you already know, is *not* what Adam Troy (Gardner McKay) used to haul on *Adventures in Paradise,* but the infantile infatuation with one's own uh-uh's. If discovered in time, the doo-doo dabbler may be diverted to modeling clay and an interest in the plastic arts. In fact, the noted sculptor Brancusi privately referred to his most famous work as *Turd in Space* and often remarked on the striking similarity between Michelangelo's *Pietà* and a big pile of dingleberries.[2]

Closely allied to feces-fiddling is another interesting bowl game known as . . .

CHAPTER 3

Operation Turdwatch, or Return of the Black Banana

There are some of you sitting at home right now who will deny ever having actually even *looked* at it. Even once. But who can resist the impulse, when flushing, to follow that long hypnotic spiral down to the Other Place? Frankly, does a more suspenseful moment exist in daily life than wondering if it will . . . aarrrgggh . . . *come bobbing back to you?*

This is no laughing matter. In Victorian times, more than one society hostess found herself cruelly brownlisted for the presence of a single anonymous "floater" in her footbath. To overcome such unreasoning squeamishness in yourself, get to know your plumbing on nonverbal levels with such Esalen-developed techniques as "commode-hugging," and invite that little nerd in the miniature sailboat out for a breath of fresh air. Lastly, remember that even the fabulous Kohinoor Diamond was once a homely lump of coal, and the way things are going lately, yesterday's breakfast might well be the President of tomorrow.

Actually, while we're in the neighborhood, let's touch for a moment[3] on your rosebud, it's care and cleaning. *Scorch marks, flash burns, skid marks, brown outs* . . . whatever you called them, carelessly hidden underwear could once make you the laughingstock of the dorm, but no more! There is no social stigma connected with this familiar household disaster. Just make sure you don't get fresh ones out of my drawer. I will kill you. I mean it.

---

[2] See also C. Brancusi, *The Phlegmish Painters: One Wop's Opinion* (New York: Random House, 1965); *idem, The Clinker in Art* (New York: Random House, 1967).

[3] And only for a moment, sickie.

CHAPTER 4

"If you pick it, it'll never heal." —Earl Scruggs

Looking for something slightly kinkier? Try scab-farming. You know, worrying that big scrumptious four-by-four-inch playground knee injury. Never letting it alone.

Scab-farmers roughly divide themselves into two schools. The first allows his boo-boo to ripen slowly until it can be picked at peak maturity. "Winter wheat" enthusiasts, however, prefer to harvest the same patch repeatedly, knowing that festering green corruption below is capable of multiple (though admittedly decreasing) yields. The first technique requires great patience and, should reaping be delayed too long, may lose the entire crop through sudden and massive flaking. Picking too soon, however, is equally chancy and may ruin the knees of your new khakis.

Those who have mastered the "winter wheat" method may wish to graduate to tick bites. Natural, long-lasting anticoagulants on the little fellow's fangs can keep your wound putrefying month after month, and if properly tended and cultivated, a single bite can produce enough sloughings to fill a pint basket!

Had enough yet? No? I'm so numb by now I can just keep on typing, but don't blame me if *you* just pick at your supper tonight.[4]

Peeling is related practice. Everyone, of course, has experienced the wordless bliss of despoiling the lifeless hulks of summer blisters, but how many of us have acquired the skill to *not go too far?* It takes a sharp eye and a steady hand, and it's not for amateurs.

Perhaps the commonest form of erotic self-mutilation is finger-eating. Not mere nail-biting, but honest-to-God finger-eating. (A correctly eaten finger should, after extended immersion in the bath, closely resemble a flayed stalk of albino broccoli.) An alternative form of such self-abuse is palate-stripping. This rather baroque reversion requires only your mouth and a ball of hard candy. As any child knows, a ball of hard candy, when sucked with enough masochistic inten-

---

[4] Or get blown by a piranha.

sity, quickly deteriorates into a mass of jagged, razor-sharp edges which score and gouge out little runnels of flesh from the roof of your mouth. For an added treat, once the candy is gone, you can vie with playmates for longest skin streamer!

CHAPTER 5

"A dog never smells his own." —Hopi proverb
"Pui est-ce qu'a coup le fromage?"—François Villon
"Softee, but deadly." —Lao-tzu

If you like to smell your farts, smile. That settled, you can come out of the water closet and dive right into some elegant spin-offs of this entertaining blast from the past. While repressed peers still stifle them against the upholstery, blush profusely, or try to frame somebody else, accomplished whiffers exist in a rarefied atmosphere where, as Father Flannegan often chuckled, there is no such thing as an ill wind.

While flatulence between consenting adults is still illegal in many states, literally millions of young moderns are finding self-realization in simple games such as the "Dutch Oven," *i.e.*, pooting in bed and *sticking your little brother's head under the covers.* The modified "Dutch Oven," commonly known as the "Besemer Furnace" or the "Wolf-Spider's Revenge," involves stepping on a frog in the hall closet, then pouncing on a member of the family and locking them inside until all sounds of struggling have ceased. Sound like fun? Try it and see! (You'll be glad you did.)

Whiffers, however, are by no means restricted to their own olfactory whistles. Women, for example, have told me in confidence that they often sample their used paper ponies, and who is to say that these fine Americans, many of them successful professionals in their chosen fields, are to be branded as "sick" or "twisted"? Besides me, I mean.

Whiffers, the legendary descendants of the first seat sniffer and the first bubble snapper, are found in all walks of life. Many respected businessmen and high government officials, under the guise of "seeing what time it is," *deliberately smell under their watches.* Golda Meir, in her autobiography, remembers that as a small pig in Milwaukee she used to lick her kneecap to *perfectly reproduce the odor of sour milk.*

Billy Kidd, the famous skier, is often photographed smelling the inside of his turtleneck, and for centuries Eskimos have occasionally put their hooded parkas on backwards "by accident" *to smell the backs of their own heads!*

Sometimes sexual reverts find themselves straddling the line between two forms of reversion. Pee-freaks' "checking the oil" have much in common with whiffers in that, after having achieved micturition, pee-freaks *smell* their trigger fingers to see whether they *really* need washing. Pee-freaks may be easily recognized as the ones who liked to perform "visiting fireman" or "fighter plane" from a standing position. (You are the fighter plane. Mission: destroy that flotilla of Daddy's cigarette butts! Buddabuddabuddabudda!)[5]

CHAPTER 6

"My wife has a little asshole. Me." —Napoleon Bonaparte

Napoleon didn't really say that. I lied. My buddy Peter Ivers says it all the time, but he lives in L.A. and probably won't know how I ripped it off, so fuck him. He also does things like throw his arm around a parking timer and say, "Hey, I got a new girl friend. Wanna meter?" or "Hey, didja hear about the big party? It's in your mouth—*everybody's* coming!"

Jesus, he's funny. I really wish you could meet him. Then I could stop pounding this cocksucker and go check out that recipe for fish oil surprise in the new *Oui.* . . .

By the way, I saw *Last Tango in Paris* finally, and I, for one, thought that the languorous pacing combined with the semi-improvisational characterizations and tactical naturalism really bit the bag. Didn't like her tits, either. (I find big tits oddly threatening, don't you?) The butter-bugger was O.K., though.[6]

[5] Tinkle Tip: If your urinal is big enough to share with a pal, why not try an impromptu "swordfight"? Just remember not to touché the Snoopy poster, the *Jokes for the John* book, or unless you're really ready for it, each other.

[6] Word has just come from the tube that NASA thinks Jupiter may actually be a giant, severed testicle. Any of you honchos lose something?

CHAPTER 7

"A people's song in a nation's heart. A nation's heart in a child's eyes. A person's foot in his little brother's sneaker by accident. Ouch." —Dag Hammarskjöld

"I am as the sound of one clam humping." —T.S. Eliot

"Officer! I think someone just sucked off my Seeing Eye dog!" —Al Hibbler

One last thing. Snowstorms. You will need: a dark-colored or black piece of construction paper, a light-colored crayon, and a near-fatal head of dandruff. What you do is, while you're waiting for Miss Walker to pass out the paste, draw a little woodland scene on your paper with your crayon, with a log cabin and a chimney on top. Then, lean your head over the paper and give yourself a double Indian-burn. Real hard. As your scalp flakes off, a beautiful winter scene will appear as if by magic. When your little scene is completely snow-bound, and if it's a first-period class, beginning about, say, 6:45 A.M. or so, you may wish to add a festive miniature snowman made from three graduated balls of eyegorp.

Another interesting finding from the Federal Drug Report was that long-term use of marihuana "greatly erodes an individual's drive, general attentiveness, sense of responsibility, and pride in appearance. He lacks get-up-and-go, and has difficulty in completing his work, turning in assignments half-

(continued on page 319)

LOUMYANS

94

SEX Through the Ages[1]

A Historie of Ye Know What, & Howe It Grewe

by Richard Armour

Sex has come to loom so large in modern society that it seems timely to consider its origins and examine it in historical perspective. The survey that follows touches only the high spots.[2] It is hoped that this brief study will open the way to further exploration by psychologists, sociologists, sexologists, and publishers of pornography.

The word *sex* comes from the Latin *sexus*, meaning division, and is akin to the verb *secare*, to cut.[3] From this it may be gathered that it takes two to make sex. In the Biblical account of the Creation, as long as Adam was the only human being on earth, there was no incentive to discuss Adam's maleness, his libido, birth control, or the constitutionality of sex education. The cutting part of Adam (see *secare*, above) to remove a rib and make of it a creature named Eve was the beginning of sex as we know it today.

Eve's eating of the Forbidden Fruit did not, therefore, create sex, only the awareness of it. "I was unaware of sex before," Eve said to Adam. Adam, who was listening none too closely and thought she said "underwear," suddenly realized that they were both stark naked.[4]

[1] Fourteen to eighty.

[2] Some of which respond interestingly to the touch.

[3] In French, sexe is a four-letter word, and therefore more titillating.

[4] The folk belief that babies are brought by the stork probably had its origin in the confusion of a "stork, naked" and "stark naked." The latter is the condition in which babies are usually conceived and invariably born.

Instead of turning tail, however, Adam turned tailor. He deftly fashioned for himself a leaf-weight suit, suitable for year-round wear in Eden. How he managed to keep it on, this being before the invention of Scotch tape, still perplexes fashion designers and structural engineers. It may have had something to do with Adam's underpinning, though any pinning over or under had to be done with exquisite care and a steady hand.

SEX IN EGYPT

Egypt lies on both sides of the Nile River. But the ancient Egyptians, as archaeologists have discovered, were not wont to lie on their sides so much as on their backs. This probably should tell us something about their sex life, at least that of their mummies. It was a fertile land.

What went on behind the pyramids we can only imagine. Graffiti were cunningly written in hieroglyphics so that tourists would not know and be embarrassed. In the early nineteenth century, however, a translation was made by Rosetta Stone.[5] It seems that the Pharaohs were half god and half man, roughly corresponding to Upper and Lower Egypt. Had the Pharaohs been all god, there is no telling what this would have done to their sex lives.

The sex goddess of ancient Egypt was Cleopatra. She mostly sat around in a gauzy skirt and a brass bra, planning conquests. Her first was Julius Caesar, a man about thirty years her senior. He was stout and balding and had little to commend him but his being an emperor, whereas she was only a queen. He carried her off to Rome, together with other spoils and spoiled her.

Her second noteworthy conquest was of Mark Antony. When they met, in 42 B.C., after the battle of Philippi, she was dressed as Aphrodite, the Greek goddess of love. Antony, who knew his mythology and had an eye for cleavage, took the hint. The fact that he was married did not stop him. After all, his wife was back in Rome and he was in Asia Minor on business and wondering what to do on weekends.[6]

[5] Née Rose Stein.
[6] Another precedent being set. See Arthur Miller's *Death of a Salesman*.

Cleopatra came to a bad end, as do some women (but not all) who play around with married men. She secured an asp, which in those days you could get without a prescription, and coaxed it to give her a poisonous bite. At first, when she placed it on her arm, the asp refused to do her bidding. But when she placed it against her breast, the asp thought to himself (he was a male asp), "Oh, what the heck!"[7]

SEX AMONG THE GREEKS AND ROMANS

The Greeks were great lovers of beauty, and it is hard to believe that they admired only friezes and urns. It was an age of manliness, and Greeks were always quick to show their prowess. Though this was long before Freud, there can be no doubt that Greek pillars had a function beyond that of holding up pediments. The Greeks, fond as they were of symbolism, were trying to tell us something.

The Greek gods should have been above carnal lust, but Zeus was forever putting on a disguise and going after some innocent young maiden.[8] Sex was not only extramarital but extrahuman. A beautiful young woman who had not been ravished by a god or two must have had little to talk about to her masseuse.

And the Spartans were not practicing physical culture just to fight better. They might sleep on a bed of nails—but not *every* night.

As for the Romans, one need only examine a painting or tapestry of the *Rape of the Sabine Women,* looking closely at the details, to realize that when Roman men went out to get wives, they were impatient with any long period of courting. They knew what they wanted[9] and wasted no time getting it. Anyhow, the Sabine women didn't have to accept Romulus'

[7] For further details about Cleopatra's sex life, see the author's *It All Started with Eve.*

[8] The time he dressed up as a bull and carried off Europa, he was really in character.

[9] The buxom type.

invitation to the festival. They must have known what was going to happen after the Romans had had a few drinks.[10]

Borrowing from the Dionysian rites of the Greeks, the Romans developed the orgy to a high point of eating, drinking, and unadulterated sex. Interestingly, the word *orgy* goes back to the Greek *ergon,* meaning work. Had you told this to a Roman lying on his back while a beautiful slave-maiden dropped grapes into his mouth, he would have snorted something like "You call this work?"[11]

Had Roman women declined more, Rome would have declined less.

SEX IN THE MIDDLE AGES

Sex in the Middle Ages was governed by the code of chivalry. This meant that anything a knight could do without getting off his horse *(cheval)* was all right. If, in addition, he kept on his suit of armor, he was trustworthy (or rustworthy), honorable, and ingenious.[12]

A knight could win a woman's favor by going on a pilgrimage, winning a joust or slaying a dragon. Having done any of the three, he would present himself to his lady fair and ask, "Prithee, milady, how about those favors?" The lady would drop a glove, and maybe, at the same time, her eyes. If the knight failed to catch them, she would be chaste.[13]

An exception was Chaucer's Wife of Bath, who was not the kind to postpone anything good. She had five husbands and could hardly wait for the sixth, wondering whether he could teach her anything new about what, in one of her more ladylike moments, she called "the olde Daunce."[14]

[10] I have carefully examined the expressions on the faces of the Sabine women in one of the famous paintings of this event, and have come to the conclusion that it was not rape.

[11] However, one definition of work is, "exertion of strength or faculties for the accomplishment of something."

[12] A medieval maiden carrying a can opener was probably not thinking of protecting herself.

[13] And sometimes she was caught.

[14] Actually, she knew all the steps, from first to last, and was more likely to give lessons than to take them.

Despite the code of chivalry, this an era of dirty stories, or *Canterbury Tales*. Almost any story involving natural or unnatural sex relations could be told in mixed company—even in front of monks, friars, parsons, and prioresses. In fact, these men and women of the cloth listened the most attentively, since this was their only way of learning about sex.[15]

The sex symbol of the Middle Ages was Queen Guinevere, who was admired by all the knights of King Arthur's court. They all wished they had her, and some, like Lancelot, managed.

SEX IN THE ELIZABETHAN AGE

The sex symbol of the Elizabethan Age was Queen Elizabeth. Her contribution to the history of sex was her ability to remain a virgin—or, more accurately, to be called the Virgin Queen—despite Sir Walter Raleigh's every attempt to worm his way into the picture.[16]

The Elizabethan poets sang lustily of sex. Consider such lines as Spenser's "A gentle knight was pricking on the plain" in *The Faerie Queene*, and, in the same poem, his description of Una, a lovely lady with "an Ass more white than snow." For a nasty sort of perversion, think for a moment[17] about John Donne's "Get with child a mandrake root." This is almost as dirty as Ben Johnson's impudent question in *The Triumph of Charis:* "Have you tasted the bag of bee?"

Shakespeare, a product of the Elizabethan Age, was always leering at lovers in compromising situations.[18] In *Hamlet,* for example, he has Polonius say of the prince, "How pregnant his replies are." Better, Hamlet's replies, than his daughter, at any rate. On another occasion, Ophelia comes right out and

[15] Do you honestly believe this?

[16] The sex play of Sir Walter's placing his cloak in a puddle and letting the queen trample on it is obviously some rare form of fetishism. So, also, no doubt, was her having Sir Walter's head cut off, something that gave her great satisfaction. (See the Marquis de Sade.)

[17] About as long as anyone can stand.

[18] Some anti-Stratfordians believe that Shakespeare was actually King Lear, or vice versa.

says to her father, regarding Hamlet, "I denied him access to me." She may have posted a sign saying "Do Not Enter Here" or "Road Closed."

Nor did Shakespeare limit his bawdiness to young lovers. In *The Taming of the Shrew*, he describes married sex in such a way to set matrimony back at least a hundred years. And then, in his *Sonnets*, he tells of his own love for a dark lady and a dark laddy. Apparently it didn't matter which sex, as long as it was dark.[19]

SEX IN THE SEVENTEENTH AND EIGHTEENTH CENTURIES

For almost 200 years, during the Age of Mistresses, sex was dominated by the French. The only blemish in what might have been an unbroken record of illicit sex was Louis XIV's marriage to his mistress, Madame de Maintenon. Cautious about such an unorthodox and un-French act, Louis delayed until he was nearly fifty. Even then, he kept the marriage secret for fear of ridicule from members of his court. Louis XIV is called the Sun King, but some scholars think this is an error caused by a reportorial or typographical slip, and that it should be Fun King.

Louis XV, who came to the throne when he was only five years old, was not at once given a mistress. "Play with these for a while," he was told, and for several years he had to get his kicks by pulling up the dresses of dolls and manikins.[20] But with completion of his puberty rites,[21] he was considered able to handle a mistress. His first, a living doll, was Madame de Pompadour. With remarkable endurance, she lasted for twenty years, perhaps because she could now and then hide in one of the hundreds of rooms of Versailles and recuperate. Madame de Pompadour was followed by Madame Du Barry. It is worth noting that when Louis first met her, she was the mistress of the Comte Jean Du Barry. Louis arranged her

[19] The principle, according to modern sexologists, is that the less you see, the more you feel.

[20] To look at their fanikins.

[21] "I demand my rites!" he shouted, meaning that he was old enough for the real thing.

100

marriage to the brother of Du Barry, since it was considered more respectable to have a married woman for mistress.[22]

SEX IN THE NINETEENTH CENTURY

The nineteenth century was a confusing and contradictory period. The same century that produced Queen Victoria produced Havelock Ellis, Baron Richard von Krafft-Ebing, and Sigmund Freud. So far as sex is concerned, this was a period of—dare we use the word?—flux.[23] Imagine, if you can, Queen Victoria on a couch and Dr. Freud seated nearby with a pen and notebook. Indeed, imagine Queen Victoria on a couch. Usually she is sitting up very straight in a straight chair, her skirt touching the floor and her legs crossed or held tightly together.

"Don't look," she would tell Prince Albert, "I am getting undressed." Whereupon she would take off her hat and gloves.[24]

Ellis and Krafft-Ebing wrote about sex from the standpoints, respectively, of psychology and neurology. By using technical language and pretending to be scientific, they managed to escape censorship. It was Havelock Ellis who wrote: "Without an element of the obscene there can be no true and deep aesthetic or moral conception of life. . . . It is only the great men who are truly obscene." This was a new way of measuring greatness. Even Thomas Bowdler would have found it difficult to expurgate the works of Shakespeare had he read such a statement.[25]

Sigmund Freud, the father of modern psychiatry, believed that sex was at the root of everything.[26] Had it not been for Freud, we might now tell our dreams to anyone who would listen instead of only to a highly paid professional. But for

[22] In discussing sex in the seventeenth and eighteenth centuries, I have left out the Puritans of New England. Does anyone mind, really?

[23] Typesetters are not always to be trusted.

[24] Prince Albert would take off, too—for Afghanistan.

[25] Bowdler died twenty-four years before Havelock Ellis was born. A physician, Bowdler must have known the facts of life, but he saw no reason for others to learn about them.

[26] This may be why some consider sex dirty.

Freud, also, we might think that a small boy's affection for his mother was rather sweet, not knowing that he had an Oedipus complex and required therapy.

Freud made it possible for people to speak knowingly about the ego, superego, and id. Previously, they had thought id was an abbreviation of *idem* and somehow related to *ibid.*

SEX TODAY

A relaxed attitude toward sex began shortly after World War I. Even the Kaiser, living in exile in Holland, began to take things easier, removing his helmet while making love.[27]

Ernest Hemingway, Gertrude Stein, Alice B. Toklas, and other members of the Lost Generation found themselves. They found themselves in Paris, living the life of artists in *pensions, ateliers,* and *pissoirs.* Writers came to grips with life, and some, who had just moved in, came to life with grips. Artists painted nudes, being too poor to afford drawing paper. It was one of those fortuitous confluences in history: Paris was full of Americans who had the money and Parisians who had the know-how.[28] Something was sure to come of it.[29]

Repeal of Prohibition had its effect on sex. A plentiful supply of liquor made it possible for a young man to ply a young woman with drink (rather than pliers) until she was completely pliable. A man was forever lifting his glass and saying, "Here's how," even though the woman he was addressing[30] needed no instructions, perhaps having been to Paris herself. However, as the Gilded Age drew to a close, it became fashionable for a man to drink out of a glass instead of a lady's slipper, and this was a blow to shoe fetishists.

Talking pictures also had their impact. Movie stars no longer had bee-stung lips,[31] and began to speak for themselves,

[27] It was a fair trade. He would take off his helmet if the girl would take off her wooden shoes. Once a young Dutch girl mistakenly sat on his helmet and it almost sent her through the ceiling.

[28] Not only the know-how but the can-can.

[29] Gonorrhea, for instance.

[30] Or undressing.

[31] Thus throwing millions of bees out of work.

saying such things as "Yes." Love scenes became more realistic. A woman's pants could now be heard as well as seen.

The stock-market crash of 1929 had its effect on sex also. Men jumped out of windows, and not always because the woman's husband had come home unexpectedly. To offset the effects of the Great Depression, women began to get shots of silicone in their breasts, and men began to feel there was still something to live for.[32]

World War II saw the use of the pinup photo to make men forget the horrors of combat. Their imaginations were raised to such a pitch that they began to think the girl waiting for them at home looked like Rita Hayworth or at least would serve the purpose. They were driven almost insane by the desire to pin down what was pinned up.

Sex made a great leap forward with the famous nude photograph of Marilyn Monroe, who did more not only for sex but for the calendar than anyone since Pope Gregory XIII.[33] Men are known to have looked at a calendar with Marilyn's photograph on it to see what day of the month it was until the day they were looking up the date for was yesterday.

We now have such sex queens as Raquel Welch and Elizabeth Taylor.[34] With them, sex has reached new dimensions.

Young people learn about sex early. Some learn about it from their parents, some from their teachers, and some from child molesters. Having had enough theorizing, many young people go to college to get firsthand (or whatever) experience by living in coeducational dormitories or cohabitational apartments.[35]

Hippies learn about sex without going to school. Mostly they lie around naked, playing with their beads.

Mention should also be made of the Pill.[36]

Nudity is now very much with us. As someone has said, "Genitalia are big." With nude men and women simulating[37]

---

[32] Science has not yet been able to do anything comparable for men.

[33] Gregory did a lot for the calendar but very little for sex. Had he posed in the nude for his own calendar, he would now be even better known.

[34] Queen Elizabeth II is not a sex queen, or even a very sexy queen.

[35] Girls living in the latter are known not as coeds but as cohabs.

[36] All right, it has been mentioned.

[37] And stimulating.

the sex act on the stage, it is no longer necessary to strain to look through a keyhole or under a window blind. A Peeping Tom is now a man who sits in the front row with a pair of binoculars.

Or he may stay home, sitting up close to the television set and watching the girls in the commercials soaping themselves in a shower or begging, with half-closed eyes and throaty voice, "Take it off. Take it *all* off."[38]

It should be apparent, as we reach the end of this brief history of sex, that forms, manners, and devices have differed somewhat through the centuries. There were, for instance, no TV cameras at the Roman orgies, nor were there minitogas. Similarly, with the advent of see-through dresses, chastity belts are "out." But such things, looked at *sub specie aeternitatis,* are seen to be superficial and transitory.

One conclusion is inescapable. The more things change, the more sex remains the same.

[38] No kidding.

Comics
by
Ed Subitzky

MÖBIUS STRIP COMICS!

PRINTER'S STRIKE COMICS!

> WANNA HEAR A SUPER ONE? THIS TRAVELLING SALESMAN COMES TO A FARMHOUSE AND LIKE HE NEEDS A PLACE TO SLEEP...

> ...SO THE FARMER SAYS HE CAN SLEEP NEXT TO HIS BEAUTIFUL DAUGHTER! AND HE TELLS HER TO YELL "TROLLEY CAR" IF HE TRIES ANYTHING!

> HAT IGHT, H ARMER UDDENLY HE RS "TURBO-TRA N" SO H RUSH S VER A D GUE S WHA HE SEE ?

THE END

COME-TOO-SOON COMICS!

THE ADVENTURES OF
TIMMY TAYLOR
IN TITLAND!

ONE MORNING, AS YOUNG BACHELOR TIMMY TAYLOR WAKES UP...

CLOSER, BABY, CLOSER! BOY DO I LOVE YOUR TITS!

SUDDENLY TIMMY REALIZES...

WAIT A MINUTE! WHAT IS THIS? I DIDN'T GO TO SLEEP WITH ANYBODY LAST NIGHT!

MY GOD! THEY'RE ON MY PILLOW! MY PILLOW HAS TITS!

SO DOES MY BED! AND MY ALARM CLOCK! AND EVERYTHING ELSE IN THE ROOM!

GASP! EVEN MY ROOM ITSELF HAS TITS!

QUICKLY, TIMMY RUSHES OUTSIDE!

EXCUSE ME, SIR, BUT WHERE AM I?

WHY, TITLAND, OF COURSE!

TIMMY TRIES TO RESIST BUT...

IT'LL BE THE GREATEST HANDFUL IN HISTORY! I'M TOO WEAK..

HUH? WHERE AM I? WHY I'M BACK IN MY BEDROOM! AND NOTHING HAS TITS! IT WAS ALL ONLY A DREAM... 'THE GREATEST WET DREAM IN HISTORY!

BUT WAIT! THERE'S SOMETHING ON MY PILLOW... IT WASN'T HERE LAST NIGHT...

IT LOOKS LIKE...

... "MOTHER'S MILK..."

? THE END

ORIGAMI COMICS!

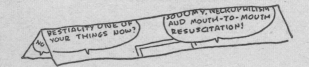

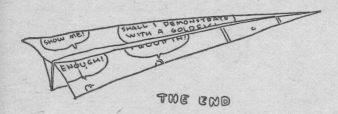

THE END

SEVEN STORIES
by
Chris Miller

Stacked Like Me

The women's movement had intrigued me from its inception. Could things really be as bad out there as the sisters were saying? My male friends pooh-poohed this notion. "That women's lib is just a bunch of dyke agitators," they explained. Yet I wondered.

I sat alone in my New York apartment one night last March, pondering. A chill breeze parted my curtains, carrying with it the bouquet of fresh dog wastes. "Shit," I thought, "the only way to find out for sure is to *become* a woman."

I decided I would do this.

I chose San Francisco as the logical starting place for my experiment. Was it not the City of Love, the very birthplace of Consciousness III? If women were free and equal anywhere, would it not be here? Ultimately, was it not the only city in the United States containing a doctor who would inject my chest with silicone?

"I'll bet I'm the only guy in the country who still does this," the doctor remarked, slipping a hypodermic beneath my left nipple as if trying to pry loose a bottle cap. "The cops would like to get me but good."

"Can you make me fairly . . . Rubenesque?" I asked.

"Fella, give me two weeks and I'll have you lookin' like Blaze Starr." He nudged me slyly and switched nipples.

In my hotel room I began learning the rudiments of femininity. I practiced the application of makeup, tried on mini-, midi-, and maxi-skirts, rehearsed sitting down and crossing my legs. My hair was already long; I now learned how to style it. I had never realized how complex a process this was. It took an hour merely to figure out the difference between conditioner and rinse. Then it developed that I had split ends. But by the end of the first day I had actually gotten my hair to swing and bounce every time I turned my head, just like in the Clairol commercials. Pleased, I went to bed. So far, woman stuff was kind of fun.

I would rue this early naïveté. Following my third set of shots, I had to begin wearing a training bra. It hurt. Garter belts were uncomfortable and the little clip things pulled my leg hairs. As the novelty of applying makeup wore off, the fun of learning a new skill was replaced by a pained awareness that for women this wasn't a game. They actually had to put stuff on their faces 365 days a year, year after year, all the while keeping track of the steady stream of new stuff being regularly released by the cosmetics companies. And the decisions! Which lipstick was blotproof? Should I wear false eyelashes on my lower eyelids, or just on the upper? Was there really a foundation that would conceal without covering? What the hell did "hypoallergenic" mean? No, achieving femininity was no cup of tea. To further complicate matters, exhaustive reading of back issues of *Sisterhood Newsletter*, *Rags*, and *Cosmopolitan* indicated the women themselves were confused about the true nature of femininity.

One thing that seemed to link all women, however, was the ritual of menstruation. I resolved to experience for myself, at least approximately, this most universal of all feminine activities. Ironically, for I did not yet appear female, that decision led to my first gut contacts with male sexist oppression.

Though I had memorized the brand names of all our nation's various menstrual devices, *Cosmopolitan* had indicated that girls in the know preferred "tampons" and that only older, uptight women still used sanitary napkins. I went to a small drugstore and, accordingly, asked the clerk for Tampax.

"Ya want the regular, the junior, or the super?" he said loudly. Behind me in line, several young men in motorcycle jackets began to snigger and nudge one another.

"The . . . super, please."

He slapped the unmistakable blue package down before me and took my money. Ears flaming, I quit the store, eyes averted from the now guffawing toughs. I felt embarrassed, intimidated, repressed . . . repressed! Males had repressed me!

Happily, I returned to my room, where I opened the package and thoroughly read the instruction folder.

Feh!

Oh, well. I withdrew a tampon, placed the Vaseline near at hand, and seated myself on the toilet. Relax and take your time, the instructions had advised. All right. I generously greased my coal shute, relaxing and taking my time.

Some time later, still breathing heavily, I got back to the tampon, which proved to be a short cylinder of absorbent cottony material contained in a pair of telescoping cardboard tubes with a string hanging from one end. It looked like an exploding party favor.

With much twisting, bending, and cheek-spreading, I finally got it up my ass and pressed the inner plunger tube, extruding the tampon snugly into my colon. It felt like a soft, unobtrusive thermometer. Soon I had forgotten all about it.

I spent the rest of the day studying the moves and gestures of women on television, paying particular attention to *A Brighter Day, Search for Tomorrow,* and commercials for detergents. About six o'clock I felt a bowel movement coming on. Not until I was seated on the toilet did I remember the alien matter blocking my rectum. If I recalled the instructions correctly, the string was supposed to be hanging out of me. I ran a finger up the smile of my bum. No string. Growing alarmed, I snatched the instruction folder from the trash. One of the "Answers to Questions New Users Sometimes Ask" said: "In a squatting position, the tampon withdrawal cord is always within reach of the fingers." Very well, I squatted and probed. Yes, there was the string—the little rascal had crawled right up inside me! Greatly relieved, for the need to take my dump was now fierce, I gave the cord a sharp tug. It pulled free easily. The tampon, however, stayed where it was.

I won't get into the details of what followed. Suffice to say that it took an hour of hard work with pliers and a kitchen fork before I had unplugged my exhaust. If a *woman* had designed that erstwhile tampon, I told myself angrily, this never would have happened. Shoddy design of menstrual aids was a more subtle facet of male repression than the tauntings of the drugstore toughs, but repression nonetheless. I was beginning to understand.

As the treatments continued, part of me began to resist my onrushing womanhood. I found myself avidly following televised football and scouring the downtown pornography shops, realizing that soon I would voluntarily forfeit these male prerogatives. Increasingly, I came to cherish my time in public men's rooms. When no one was looking, I swore and spat.

But my womanhood was becoming harder and harder to ignore. I was acquiring quite a set of jugs, for one thing. Obviously I couldn't let myself be noticed while in sexual midstream, but how might I reasonably hide myself?

The solution was as simple as it was inspired—a life vest! I purchased a large, military-surplus "Mae West" and, chuckling inwardly all the while at the irony of the appellation, began wearing it everywhere save my hotel room. To those who asked, I explained that I feared the San Andreas Fault.

"I'd make this the last set of injections if I were you," advised the doctor. "Those knockers are already big enough to drive someone up to his ankles in the pavement."

I looked down at myself. Indeed, I had become what the Jewish faith calls *zoftig*. The nipples were a little underdeveloped, perhaps, but that was a minor consideration. Undeniably, I was built like a brick you-name-it.

The doctor now injected my vocal cords with *striacaine*, a tautener. When the anesthetic wore off, my new voice was high and squeaky, even "cute." Greatly pleased, I reached to wring his hand, but then remembering my new role, gave him a peck on the cheek instead.

Leaving his office, I was confronted, as usual, with the giant likeness of Carol Doda reclining with bulbous grandeur upon the marquee of the topless club across the street. "Poor oppressed sister," I thought. "I too shall know the grinding heel of the male Amerikan boot this day. From now on, I am one of you."

It took two hours and several razor blades to remove the fur from my legs, arms, armpits, and the vast new three-dimensionality of my chest. Last to go (and not without a sigh) were my moustache and sideburns.

The concealment of my rather large, substantial member was vital. I had experimented with several brands of G-string, but these delicate underthings could not suppress that telltale bulge. Now, reluctantly, I looped my genitals beneath my crotch and stuffed them between the cheeks of my buttocks, securing them there with adhesive tape.

Next, clothes. I had decided it best to dress in some inconspicuous current mode, to be "just one of the girls." Accordingly, I donned filmy black panties, tight jeans, and a "Keep On Truckin'" T-shirt. Finally, I brushed my hair and anointed each earlobe with just a trace of Shalimar.

Only then did I allow myself to look in the mirror. I blinked. Staring back at me was the face of a stranger—and not bad stuff, either! The reflection contained no hint of maleness. No, this image led back to pink frilly dresses, dolls, home ec classes, sugar and spice. I was a newly created woman, and it was time to leave the safety of my hotel room for a new life.

With extreme self-consciousness, I stepped into the street. Lunch-hour crowds surged this way and that, and at first nobody noticed me. The knife edge of my paranoia had just begun to dull, when I collided with a construction worker crossing Market Street and was knocked sprawling.

Naturally, my first instinct was to demand, "Hey, ya stupid pig bastard, where ya walkin'?" The words froze in my throat as I remembered what I was. *I wasn't allowed to talk that way anymore.* My new persona had no *idea* what to do. I grew flustered and began to hiccup.

Abruptly the great hairy arms of the man were around me and I was being lifted to my feet. Of course—passivity! And he was being a "gentleman!" Well, not bad, I thought, and went to brush myself off. It was then that I realized his arms were still around me.

Our eyes locked. I simpered. His gaze rolled down, then up, but not as far as my face. I could actually see his pupils dilate. Women friends had told me about the "lust stare"; now, in my first hour as a woman, I was receiving one. Why, the crude billy goat! I pulled free and walked rapidly away.

My first need was a job. I found an employment agency and took a seat beside the desk of a small, birdlike woman.

"Can you type?" she asked me.

"Well, no . . ."

"No openings."

It was time to test my major gambit. Fixing her with a sincere gaze, I said, "But surely there must be *something* . . . for a sister?"

"Don't give me any of that lesbian stuff," she replied. "No openings."

I sighed. "Now you're being defensive. Don't you realize that the reason we women compete with and resent each other so is that men make us despise ourselves? What we need is solidarity! Now, if you could find a job for me, it would certainly be a move toward—" I broke off as she raised her paperweight threateningly. Poor brainwashed sister. I left hurriedly.

It was late afternoon. My feet hurt and I had to pee. Everywhere I went men turned and gaped, many of them giving me the "lust stare." I began to sweat. Though perspiring had never particularly bothered me as a male, my new self was horrified. How could I be a woman and smell like a gym sock? So lonely and oppressed I felt!

At least I could do something about my bladder. I entered

a bookstore and asked the clerk the location of the rest rooms.

"Sorry, no ladies' room. Try the shoeshine parlor next door."

How sad, I thought. The man was not, of course, relating to *me* but rather to societal imperatives against my gender. Though something primitive and male in me wanted to kick his smartass nuts, I lowered my eyes submissively and walked next door.

"Could I use your señorita's room?" I asked the manager.

"¡Ay!" he replied. "¡Joo got some *tetas!* ¿Joo need job?"

"In a shoeshine parlor?" I asked, surprised.

"*Sí.* Thees a *topless* shoeshine parlor." He drew back the curtain that separated us from the interior of his emporium, and I saw a long row of sisters *shining shoes with their tits out!*

"No, thank *you!*" I spun on heel and left.

Not until some days later did I recognize the sociological validity of working in such a place. After all, I realized, where better to experience the casual minefields of moment-by-moment abasement they make you walk through when you're a woman in Uncle Sam's more-yang-than-yin pig Amerika? Moreover, as I had been unable to find other work, it was topless or starve. Returning to the shoeshine parlor, I accepted a position at a dollar a week plus tips.

They dressed me in a pert Naugahyde miniskirt and entrusted me with an empty chair. Next in line was a shoeshiner named Trixie, whose rather droopy mammae were dappled black, cordovan, and oxblood.

I gave her a small, self-deprecatory smile. "Hi, sister," I whispered.

"Don't give me any of that lesbian stuff," she replied, and refused to look at me again.

A poor start. Things got worse when my superior mammary shelf attracted long lines of men and I was made number one in the shoeshine line. Though I felt sadness at the jealousy now displayed by my sisters and shock at the extent to which they had swallowed the male line that large milk glands make you ipso facto a better person, I nonetheless accepted with gratitude the generous tips of my customers. I mean, a girl has to eat.

In the days that followed, there were other subtle shifts in attitude. At first I had resented such reminders of my second-class status as having doors held for me, my cigarettes lighted, my arm held while walking across the street. To my surprise, I soon came to like and expect these things. Crossing the street alone had always frightened me.

In almost any problem situation you can name, I found that all you have to do is look alone and helpless to attract packs of straining, helpful males. When you cross streets against the light, male drivers screech to a halt instead of running you over. You discover that you can make things happen merely by batting your eyes, which seemed to me infinitely more pleasing aesthetically than the male-preferred approach of batting one's antagonists.

I began to comprehend the subtleties of cosmetics, how lavender shadow made my eyes seem larger and Strawberry Slicker set off my nipples. Several real nice guys started buying me drinks and taking me to fancy restaurants. I had to begin diet lunches to maintain my figure.

I even came to appreciate women's rest rooms. Apparently, women have been culturally conditioned to *sit* while peeing. Of the literally hundreds of ladies' rooms I have used, *not one has contained a urinal*. At first, this enforced bending-of-the-knees made me feel degraded. Soon, I came to appreciate the opportunity to get off my dogs for a while.

And my bankroll was growing.

Things might have gone on like this indefinitely, but less than a month after beginning my job I overheard by chance a conversation that was to end my lucrative hiatus. I was sitting at a lunch counter, wishing I could allow myself something other than fruit salad and cottage cheese, when the words of two robust, amiable gentlemen seated behind me impinged on my thoughts. They were discussing the larger fellow's car and the pesky transmission that was making his life such a situation comedy.

I felt a sudden chill. My mind, filled with recipes and fashion advertising, could scarcely remember what a transmission *was*. How thoroughly my female role had taken me over! Fun was fun, but enough was enough. I decided it was time to end my little ruse, crank out a book, maybe do a couple of talk shows, then relax and take things easy for a while. I ran outside and hailed a cab.

At the doctor's office I found a debt-retrieval agency carrying off the doctor's equipment. The doctor, they told me, had left town suddenly.

Panic wove its magic fingers inextricably into my intestines. Without the doctor I would have to live the rest of my life with these fleshapoid balloons entering every room before I did. Then I remembered the redheaded stripper I had seen a few times in the doctor's waiting room. Could she know anything? It was a slim chance, but I was in no position to pass up long shots.

I found her in a dressing room at Total Nudity from Twelve Noon! At first, fearing that I was an informer in the pay of male sexist police, she wrapped her robe tightly about her and refused to tell me anything. I considered beating her bloody with my purse, but gritted my teeth and stayed in character instead.

"Wahhhhh!" I told her. "I jus' *hafta* find him."

She began to soften. "Aw, yer just a kid, aincha? Come here, honey, an' putcher head on my chest."

I went. "Awww," she said, and pulled me into her lap, laying my cheek against the freckled overswell of her left breast. My tears merged with flesh and ran in tiny trails to the vee of her robe, mingling with the natural moistures of her cleavage to emit a combined perfume that wreaked musky monkeyshines on my olfactory centers. "Awww," she crooned, and began stroking my hair. I decided to allow myself to be consoled for a while.

"You'll give me the doctor's new address then?" I asked at length in my best little-girl voice.

"Awwww," she said, and switched from my hair to my inner thigh. Beneath my miniskirt, beneath my black-lace panties, I felt alarums and excursions. An *erection?* I'd forgotten all about them! And it felt terrific! I began slowly to part her robe, marveling at the creamy pink of her nipples and the way they gathered and focused themselves beneath my fingers. Her nails trailed further my thigh.

Then, with surreal slowness, my adhesive tape began to tug loose, each tug parting a pubic hair from my scrotum with a tiny, silent pop of pain. Adhesive tape? Abruptly, I remembered my role and, in doing so, realized just what kind of woman I was dealing with.

"Don't give me any of that lesbian stuff," I said. I leaped from her lap and snatched up the purse.

"Los Angeles!" she shrieked. "Sunset and Alvarado!"

I beat it back to my hotel, packed my few things, tucked my bankroll in my panties, and started for the airport. It certainly wasn't my day. While searching for a cab, I was accosted by a large, generous-lipped third-worlder who claimed he wanted my pussy but was more than delighted to find my cash. Penniless, I was forced to hitchhike.

I was picked up immediately by a man in a suit who moved his briefcase to let me sit. We headed south. My mind whirled with plans, pique, and panic. Gradually, I became aware that my driver was talking to me. I shook my head to clear it.

"Tell me," he was asking, "is it true that women ejaculate?"

Though today I realize that his questions were merely a sad, twisted attempt to get close to me, at the time I was appalled. I moved as far away from him as I could, pressing my back to the door.

"Sorry, I don't mean to offend you. It's just that I'm curious. You see, I'm really on your side: I believe in the women's movement. Y'know?"

"Yeah, well, I'm not offended, but just knock off the sexy questions, O.K.?"

"Of course."

For a few minutes we drove in silence.

"Ah . . . I was wondering . . . if I pulled behind a gas station, would you rate the size of my penis?"

"Stop the car!"

He did. Believing that I had been picked up by an isolated nut, I began hitchhiking again. But no, there were to be more than a dozen rides, all from men, each worse than the one before. They seemed to assume that in the presence of a woman of such formidable bosom no pretense of dignity or self-respect was necessary. Some were shamelessly open ("Say, how do you stand up?"), others shamelessly subtle ("May I, heh heh, have a closer look at your love beads?"). Many breathed heavily, a few drooled. This was Man the Oppressor? In fact, this was Man? I felt contempt. I decided to try an experiment.

"Hee hee, you're cute! If you drive me all the way to Los Angeles, I'll let you jerk off between my tits."

"Gosh! You bet!"

There it was. I had sought the truth and found it, and now I felt stunned. All the while I'd thought *men* were the oppressors. But that couldn't be—not if I could make them do anything I wanted merely by inhaling. The discriminatory laws, the institutionalized condescension, the degrading lavatories . . . all must be elements of a ruse. The entire women's movement, with its bizarre rhetoric and carefully staged suggestions of incompetence, was but another element of the camouflage. While men strode about doing the work and thinking they ran things, the women sat back and coolly ran the men, *controlling them like laboratory animals with electric-pleasure promises from the grottoes of their vulvae.* Had my last driver not been so preoccupied with my knockers, he might have wondered at the cold laughter that now bubbled from the soft inviting lips of the "sex object" sitting next to him.

When we reached Los Angeles, I let the yokel have his fun, wiped myself off with the doctor's address, and threw it in a litter basket. Then I sold my credit and ID cards, my last link with my former self, to a black-market credentialist for fifty bucks. I let him bounce my boobs for a few minutes, and he made it another fifty. I put the entire sum into new clothes and a visit to the beauty parlor.

In the past year I have acquired control of three hotels, a nightclub, a bowling alley, and a small housing development. I own a Lincoln and a Bentley, and my chauffeur is an upper-class Bulgarian. I am about to open a numbered Swiss bank account.

Sisterhood is powerful.

Right on!

Mr. Rock 'n' Roll Meets the Amboy Dukes

They drove through a wilderness of concrete, bakeries, and temple youth centers, on roads with alien-sounding names like Flushing Boulevard and Utopia Parkway. Comfy, suburban Nozzlin was now just memory. The air was filled with urban reek.

Mr. Rock 'n' Roll slouched lower in the back seat of Ned's car, only his blond, James Dean-style hair and mirror sunglasses visible through the side window. He wondered if maybe he wouldn't be happier if he were home, doing his social studies assignment and listening to Dr. Jive on the radio. What had possessed him to let Ned talk him into cruising for city girls? He hadn't even achieved contact with suburban girls yet, unless you counted the furtive elbow-breast numbers he sometimes managed in the crowded halls. And yet, here he was, scanning the streets of Queens and feeling well out of his depth.

Ned, Steamin', and Stu, he knew, often cruised in search of city girls, exchanging alligator shirts and loafers for pegged pants and fruit boots in a lavatory after school and speeding off in Ned's chartreuse Henry J. To date, they had been utterly unsuccessful in their quest, but they never stopped trying. Mr. Rock 'n' Roll could understand their persistence, in a way. He, too, had admired city girls, whom he had seen many times at rock-'n'-roll shows at the Brooklyn Paramount. You could identify these urban exciters by their half-scarves, small gold crosses, and that certain aura of come-near-me-and-I'll-rip-out-your-throat. They were very sexy. But actually to go after them? To give up on the pompon-beclad Suzies and Joanies of Nozzlin, whom he hadn't gotten to first base with anyway, in favor of concealed razor-blade-carrying Angies and Doloreses? He must be out of his nut. Maybe he'd be lucky and all the city girls would be home at this hour, sharpening their teeth.

"Ooh! Ooh! There's one! Omigod, she's *gorgeous!*"

Steamin' had his face pressed against the windshield. A vein stood out at his neck. "Lookit that *scarf!*"

"I see her." Ned swung left onto 27965th Street, accelerated, and then eased off, eliciting from his car's interior a loud rumbling popping effect which he hoped would pass for a glass-pack but which actually was a hole in his muffler. The city girl walked on, seemingly oblivious to their sonic tour de force. Her white scarf knot dangled against her pin-curl clips like a small rabbit at play in barbed wire.

"Beep the horn," suggested Stu.

"Schmuck," said Ned. "That's really going to impress her, beeping the horn."

Steamin' pulled back from the windshield. In one smooth motion, like a dog catching a thrown stick, he drew his comb from his back pocket, craned to the rear-view mirror, and began straightening the line of his DA. "Weeds," he snapped. "Quick!"

Stu hurriedly passed out cigarettes. Mr. Rock 'n' Roll felt drawn into the excitement in spite of himself. He sat up straighter as they pulled abreast of the city girl. There was something irresistible in the utter indifference she exuded toward all around her. So complete was her absence of response to their presence that he wondered briefly if she weren't right, that they weren't really there at all.

Steamin' rolled down his window. "Hey! Hi!" he called smoothly.

The girl popped her gum loudly enough for them to hear it in the car. Steamin' took this to be a favorable sign.

"Hey, where yuh goin'?" he shouted seductively.

The city girl turned up a concrete walk and into a house, slamming the door behind her.

"*Shit!*" said Steamin'.

Each of Mr. Rock 'n' Roll's cruising companions had his own technique for attracting girls. Ned's was his car. True, a '51 Henry J did not have quite the evil ambience of, say, a '49 Merc, but it was the only car he was likely to own in the foreseeable future and he'd done his best to render it presentable, painting it, putting on skirts and spinners, lowering it (with a pile of bricks in the trunk), and, finally, bullnosing the hood. He had never quite figured out how to plug the two small holes left by the removal of the hood ornament and this caused the car to whistle high C at speeds exceeding thirty miles an hour, but Ned felt that this small price to pay for the added visual class. In Nozzlin, he'd been knockin' 'em dead with his car.

Stu was a dancer. At record hops, he was supreme, bopping and slopping with the toughest chicks around. Unhappily, he usually departed from these affairs alone, due to his face, which looked like a pizza, and breath, which smelled like old pus.

Steamin' relied on image. His head sported the most immaculate DA in Nozzlin High School, and his brow the most casual triangle of forehead curls. He dressed continental, with tapered black pants, tapered Italian striped shirts, tapered suede belt, and tapered-point shoes. In fact, Steamin' was tapered. His long stringy frame was perfect for slouching, leaning against walls, stretching out legs when seated, leaning over school desks so that his shirt lifted to show the small of his back, and many other cool postures. Though his image had not yet attracted quite the horde of females he'd been banking on, Steamin' knew from the way he impressed certain freshman boys that it was only a matter of time.

Mr. Rock 'n' Roll wasn't sure about his girl-attracting technique. His assumption had been that through sheer volume of listening to records he would become very cool. He had even gone so far as to memorize the label information—composer, time, catalog number, and dance designation ("fox-trot," "calypso")—of every record he owned. The effectiveness of this technique was debatable. His usual opening gambit, "Who you like better, the Cleftones or the G-clefs?" had thus far been met only with blank stares and contemptuous giggles. It was late in the game for Mr. Rock 'n' Roll, already spring of his junior year. Not getting laid had become the very core and crux of his life. If only he, like his cruisemates, were a mean motor scooter and bad go-getter.

"A scarf!" cried Steamin'. "I see a scarf!"

"Where?"

"You missed it! Go back and turn left! Hurry!"

Ned wheeled the car around, its lowered rear scraping a curb abrasively.

"Hurry!" Steamin' was almost shouting. "She was way down the street from here!"

Ned peeled out, leaving rubber. Mr. Rock 'n' Roll, impressed, felt that *this* city girl would *have* to dig them.

"There! Stop! Stop!"

"Where?" demanded Stu.

"Oh, `fuck!`" said Steamin'.

Outside was a mailbox with a scarf tied around its flag.

Mr. Rock 'n' Roll contemplated his forearms and sighed. Even clenching his fists, he could barely see his veins, and how puny they looked compared to the mighty road maps he had observed on the forearms of hoods. Of Mr. Rock 'n' Roll's friends, only Steamin' had good forearm veins, but Mr. Rock 'n' Roll knew that these resulted less from proletarian virility than from the tight rubber bands Steamin' wore about his armpits. Effective, though.

The Henry J rolled on. Mr. Rock 'n' Roll began to wonder when they would be going home. It was becoming night and Ned had only a junior license. Police had injected teen-agers' testes with turpentine for less. He was about to raise this point when two girls with scarves undulated from an oncoming candy store.

"Holy shit!" cried Steamin'. "Pull over! Pull over!"

Ned decelerated to a crawl. The two girls were prime types, from the sullen expertise with which they sucked upon their cigarettes to the cornucopias of rejection implicit in the down-turned corners of their mouths. They even had just the right amount of skin trouble so that just the right amount of too much makeup was necessary. The faint crusting effect was devastating.

"Hey! Watcha doin'?" Steamin' inquired.

The girls turned to look at them. This had never happened before. Steamin' was dumbstruck. He shot a desperate look at Ned.

"Ah . . . whatcher names?" said Ned.

Mr. Rock 'n' Roll had all he could do to keep from sinking below window level. He knew the retorts to this question. "What's it to ya?" was one, or "Giddadahere or I'll get my boyfriend to kick the shit outtaya."

"My name's Connie," said the blond city girl, "and this is Darlene." Her brunette companion regarded them with hot eyes. "What's *yer* names?"

Steamin' recovered his aplomb. "Oh, uh, this is Vinnie and Joe and Tony," he said, indicating Ned, Stu, and Mr. Rock 'n' Roll. "And I'm Angelo. Uh . . . how'd ya like ta? . . ."

"Sure," said Connie, and the girls squeezed into the car, Connie between Ned and Steamin', and Darlene, cringing slightly from Stu, in warm thigh contact with Mr. Rock 'n' Roll.

Stu, flustered, hazarded a few dance steps. Attempted in the back seat of a crowded Henry J, these moves made him look like a demented man Mr. Rock 'n' Roll had once seen on a subway. Darlene inched farther from him, pressing Mr. Rock 'n' Roll with soft firmness.

"Where you from, Tony?" she asked him.

"Well, originally I was from Brooklyn, but when I was six we moved to . . ."

"We're from Northport," said Ned quickly, pronouncing it "nawt-pawt."

"Where's *that?*" asked Connie.

"Well, if you're from Brooklyn," cooed Darlene to Mr. Rock 'n' Roll, "then how 'bout drivin' us home?"

"Oh, well, I don't really think we can. . . ."

"Why certainly we can," said Ned. "Love driving in Brooklyn." And he headed for the expressway.

Mr. Rock 'n' Roll felt defense systems collapse somewhere in his midsection. Paranoia attacked his liver. Brooklyn? Except for rock-'n'-roll shows, he hadn't been in Brooklyn since he was a little kid. All he knew about Brooklyn was that people got beaten there a lot with chains. He watched in near paralysis as Darlene nonchalantly monitored a lipstick application in the lenses of his shades.

"Yer cute, y'know?" she told him. "When we get to the clubhouse, whyntcha come in for a while?" She touched the tip of her tongue briefly to the ripe center of her upper lip.

"Listen, Darlene," said Mr. Rock 'n' Roll, "we really have to . . ."

"Fantastic!" cried Steamin'. "Love to come in for a while."

"Sure would," said Ned.

"Damn right," said Stu. "Love to come in."

Darlene took Mr. Rock 'n' Roll's hand and placed it on her knee. "Don't worry, honey," she whispered. "I don't believe in lovers' cramps."

Mr. Rock 'n' Roll swallowed with difficulty. He wasn't sure exactly what lovers' cramps were. Possible he already had a case; his lower trunk felt filled with ball bearings in Brownian movement. The deeper the car penetrated the tenement canyons of Brooklyn, the more intensely he yearned for lawn sprinklers and cocker spaniels, and the cool, linen security of his soft bed at home.

The alley that contained the clubhouse entrance appeared to have recently been struck by a garbage storm. The girls led them through a soft blanket of Kleenex and bottle caps, candy wrappers and Thunderbird bottles, to a dark rectangle in the building side. A broken, concrete stair descended to a door of rotting wood.

"It's ... perfect," breathed Steamin'.

Connie led them in. Darlene illuminated the cellar to full gloom with an ancient gooseneck lamp of the sort one might see in the front office of a seltzer factory. About the walls were mattresses upon which Mr. Rock 'n' Roll fantasized cavalcades of hot dago sexuality.

"I'll put on some music," said Darlene. She walked to a rickety table bearing a fat-spindled 45 turntable and seven thousand records.

Stu's eyes lit. He leaped to center floor, warmed up with some leg and toe moves, worked into a full slop, and concluded with a perfect Jackie Wilson split.

"I like slow songs," said Darlene, unimpressed. A Harptones ballad commenced at her last word, disc-jockey-like. Stu sank dejectedly to a mattress. The last time he had attempted to dance slow with someone, his breath had summoned from his startled partner an arc of vomit that had cleared three other couples before landing in the South Seas Punch.

"C'mon, Tony, let's fish." Darlene took Mr. Rock 'n' Roll in both arms, fitting flush against him from dimpled knee to crusty cheek. When she worked a thigh between his legs, he felt some response was called for and began to croon along with the Harptones' falsetto tenor.

"Jeez, you sing nice," sighed Darlene, and popped her gum very close to his ear.

Ned, meanwhile, was dancing with Connie, impressing her with a smooth series of dips, turns, and sudden dramatic pauses. Steamin' deigned to dance. His spasticism had been legendary since he had tripped against a display table in biology, destroying seventeen science projects. Instead, he prowled the room, emitting small cries of pleasure at the discovery of, say, a pink and black sock or a zip gun.

When the next record didn't go down, Darlene left Mr. Rock 'n' Roll to go slap the turntable into reengagement. Then she turned off the light. The sweet voices of Nolan Strong and the Diablos floated through the darkness:

> You've taken my money,
> Told me lies ...

He heard a giggle approach, then felt warm, sticky lips carom from his nose to his ear to his mouth like soft pinballs. A tongue slipped between his lips in an effulgence of Juicy Fruit. It was Mr. Rock 'n' Roll's first French kiss; perhaps he staggered a little, for Darlene now drew him to a mattress.

"Get yer vines off, honey," she whispered. "I'll be right back." Each sentence was terminated with a tongue thrust, creating small moist pops in his ear that were much like periods. Footsteps padded away; then, from across the room, he heard excited whispers from Stu and Steamin' and the tinkling of belt buckles.

In an agony of excitement, Mr. Rock 'n' Roll tugged his jeans to his ankles. He couldn't believe it, but they were actually going to get . . .

The light went on. The first thing Mr. Rock 'n' Roll saw, dangling before his eyes, was a stout length of chain. The second was a large hood, looming over him like an angry god.

They were prodded by boot toes into a pink and white huddle before a battered armchair. Arranged around the armchair were a dozen or so glowering hoods. Seated within was a blond, rangy hood with incredible forearm veins *and* a snake tattoo. Connie and Darlene were nowhere to be seen.

"O.K., what we got here, Bull?" asked the blonde of a vast-shouldered hood at his right.

"Rose and Janie brought them in, Larry," said Bull, consulting a clipboard. "Claim to be from Northport, though our auxiliary there has no knowledge of them. Using the names Vinnie, Joey, Tony, and Angelo." He turned a page. "Let's see . . . wearing collars up though middle class . . . misrolled sleeves . . . aspiring to arm veins . . . holder *filter* cigarettes . . . operating an embarrassing vehicle . . . crossing class lines with lustful intent . . . oh, and get this—wearing *Jockey* shorts!"

The hoods nudged one another, grinning.

"Anything more?" asked Larry.

"No. Except, any of you guys ever see so many circumcised cocks at one time in your life?"

The hoods sniggered.

"Shut up," said Larry. "Which one's the dancer?"

"Him," said Bull. "The one with the pizza face."

"O.K., you, on your feet. Crazy, put on a record."

"Right, Larry. Record." A huge, twitching hood limped to the record player. Stu didn't move. He had curled into a tight fetal ball between Ned and Steamin'.

"Hey, you," said Larry. "Get up and dance, or I'll tell Crazy to pull out your rib cage."

"Skoo-be-doo-be-doo," replied Stu, catapulting to his feet, popping his fingers and tapping his toes. Crazy dropped the needle onto "WooWoo Train." The Valentines lamented:

> There goes the train, oop sh sh
> Movin' down the line, oop sh sh
> Takin' my baby from me, oop sh sh

Stu was transcending himself. Never had his boogie been dirtier, nor his potatoes so mashed. At the close of the song, he spun thrice and toppled backward, catching himself with one hand and flinging himself upright again in a perfect simulation of the Valentines' own stage finale.

There was a pause. The hoods looked at one another, then at Larry.

"What you think, Crazy?" Larry asked.

"Give me his *feet!*"

"See, Crazy's got a clubfoot," explained Larry. "He wasn't never able to get the girls by snappy dancin'. He had to get a job workin' in a meat factory so's he could give the girls steaks. In return, they give him a little of *their* meat. Sometimes."

"Yeah," said Crazy. "And maybe if I give Janie one of your feet, she'll let me play with her woolly." He drew a stained butcher knife.

"Cool it, Crazy," said Larry gently. "His feet won't go away. Bull, which one's the driver?"

"The runt," said Bull.

Ned stood up slowly, holding his arms stiffly at his sides.

"O.K., Angelo or Tony or whatever your name is, tell us about the car."

"Well, it used to belong to Grandma Millie, but she died of Asian flu and my mother gave it to me. The car, I mean. Uh, I put skirts and spinners on it, bullnosed it, decked and lowered it, and I'm gonna get dual pipes as soon as I can, and . . ."

"Yeah," said Larry. "Well, guy, you see this cat behind me." He indicated a dark, pimpled hood. "Black Kenny always wanted a car, but his old man didn't even have enough bread to get one for himself. Then the war came along and Black Kenny's old man got his legs blowed off at Anzio. So the government grafted a set of wheels onto his thigh stumps and sent him home. Two weeks later, the ol' man has a flat on the West Side Highway and goes through a guard rail. Now Kenny ain't got a father *or* a car."

"Lemme have the car, Larry," begged Black Kenny. "First thing I'll do is knock off the bumper and tie the runt there instead. Then I'll drive into a wall five or six times."

"Good thought, Kenny. We'll get to it. But first, which one's the fruitcake with the rubber bands?"

"That skinny one there, Larry. The one what just passed out."

"Frank?"

A lean handsome hood with black pomaded hair unzipped his fly and emptied his bladder into Steamin's face, rapidly eroding the perfect furrows of Steamin's DA. Steamin' leaped to his feet, steamin'.

"So you wanta look tough and pretty," said Larry.

"Uh, yeah. I thought that's how yuh get the chicks." Steamin' wiped his face with his sleeves.

"Well, pretty boy, it doesn't always get the 'chicks.' Frank here's the handsomest dude on this turf. You know what it got *him*? Gang-raped contantly by Greeks from the next neighborhood. Until his cheeks fused together. Now Frank takes his dumps into a plastic bag he wears tied to his waist."

"Yeah, but I can still piss O.K., huh, guys?" observed Frank. The other hoods chuckled and popped their fingers.

"What you want to do with him, Frank?"

"How 'bout we shave his head, then cut the veins outta his arms an' fasten 'em to his skull wit' his rubber bands. Then, every time he combs his hair, he'll hafta remember how *vain* he's bein'."

The hoods fell out, slapping one another's backs and shaking their heads helplessly.

"Not bad, Frank. You got a clever head behind that pretty face and don't think we don't know it."

Mr. Rock 'n' Roll knew he was next. Through his terror, he had been conceiving a plan. It wasn't fully worked out, but it would have to do. He was so scared he felt calm.

"O.K., the record nut. Hey, James Dean. Stand up."

Mr. Rock 'n' Roll stood up.

"Dean, lemme introduce you to Hambone." He gestured toward a gangling Negro hood with a high, Little Richard do. "Hambone had one of these old ladies who's always fallin' for rock-'n'-roll stars. One week, Clyde McPhatter, the next week, Jackie Wilson, always somebody new. Hambone figured he hadda be a star too. So he worked on his voice for six months and finally landed second tenor spot with the Wrens. Naturally, his girl came to his first performance, which happened to be at a show at the Brooklyn Fox. That night, Hambone sung his heart out. Didn't you, Hambone?"

"Thass right."

"But after the show, she wasn't waiting for you at the stage door, was she?"

"She sho' wuzzin'."

"Where was she, Hambone?"

"She done run off wif Frankie Lymon an' de Teenager, *thass* where she wuz!"

"And today Hambone is a men's room attendant."

"Thass right."

The room was hushed. "What'll we do with him, Hambone?"

"Well, Ah spec we could shove de forty-five turntable up hiz ass an' scratch him wif' needles till he sing de whole rhythm an' blues top forty."

Mr. Rock 'n' Roll cleared his throat. "Just a minute," he said. "I realize you guys want to get on with this, but before you do, I'll bet you know the answer to a record question that's been bothering me for years."

"Ah, fuck that shit, Larry," said Crazy, hopping up and down on his good foot. "Let's get 'em now."

Mr. Rock 'n' Roll held his breath.

"Shit, what the hell. Go ahead, Dean, ask away."

"Well, as you all know, there were three recorded versions of 'Hearts of Stone,' not counting, of course, the insipid cover by the Fontaine Sisters. One of the originals was by the Charms, and another was by the Jewels. My question is, who did the third?"

The hoods regarded one another.

"Uh, wuz dat by de Castelles?" asked Hambone.

"No," said Mr. Rock 'n' Roll. "They sang 'Hearts of Steel.' "

"The Schoolboys?" asked Bull.

"No, they did 'Hearts of Spain.' "

The hoods began a soft rumble of questions to one another. Their eyebrows furrowed. A few scratched their heads.

"Gee," said Mr. Rock 'n' Roll. "I thought sure *you* guys would know."

"Wait a minute, wait a minute," said Larry. "We know. Just wait a minute."

"The Bopchords?"

"No, man, it was the Magnificents."

"You kiddin'? They weren't around then."

"Well how 'bout the Keynotes?"

A few at a time, the hoods began drifting to the record table to flip through handfuls of 45s. At length, only Larry and Crazy were still watching the captives.

"Now, Stu," hissed Mr. Rock 'n' Roll. "Your breath!"

Stu, quick on the uptake and nimble as the dancer he was, came to his feet expelling breath like an aerosol can. First Larry, then Crazy, went down retching.

"Let's go," cried Mr. Rock 'n' Roll, and before the startled hoods at the record table could react, the four boys had launched for the door.

"Hey! Stop! Where yuh goin'?" bellowed angry voices. A stampede of bootsteps started after them.

The boys flew up the stairs, into the alley, and hurled themselves into the Henry J. Ned hit the ignition. The motor turned over once . . . and died.

"Migod!" screamed Steamin'. "Hurry!"

The hoods were boiling up the cellar steps, sweeping toward the car. Ned tried again. *Rrr rrr rrr.* Nothing. And then the hoods were on them. Frank reached through the driver's window and grabbed Ned by the hair. Black Kenny drew a slender stiletto and held it at Ned's throat. The boys stopped breathing.

"All right, what's the answer?" asked Bull.

"Answer? Answer?" said Ned in a little squeezed-up voice.

"Don't get smart wit' us," snarled Black Kenny. "Tell us who recorded that third version of 'Hearts of Stone' or I'll stick this fuckin' blade down yer throat."

"Gnee! Gnee!" said Ned to Mr. Rock 'n' Roll. "Tell'm! Tell'm!"

"The Midnighters, 1954, on the Excello label," shouted Mr. Rock 'n' Roll, all in a rush.

"The Midnighters! Holy shit!" Frank turned to share a stunned look with Hambone.

"The Midnighters," breathed Black Kenny. "The *Midnighters!*" He pulled back from the window. "Hey, it was the Midnighters," he called to Larry and Crazy, who were emerging unsteadily from the clubhouse, their faces somewhat green.

Ned, suddenly free, twisted the key again. This time, the engine caught. Ned squeezed his eyes shut and floored the gas. With a quite respectable vroooommmmm, the Henry J. screeched from the alley. Through the rear window Mr. Rock 'n' Roll caught one last glimpse of the hoods, staring at one another and shaking their heads in grudging admiration.

"Jesus," said Ned. "Let's go home."

"Yeah," said Stu.

"I," said Steamin', "was feeling like home was a thousand miles away."

"By the Heartbeats, 1955, on the Hull label," murmured Mr. Rock 'n' Roll, and awaited at the window the return of trees.

Invisible Robkin in the Girls' Locker Room

Mr. Zobiah, the chemistry teacher, was noted for his lips. They were thin and plum-colored, and puffed when they met like gently squeezed blisters. When apart, they released generous clouds of lethal chemical breath, emissions that each year caused several of his eleventh-graders to faint dead away.

Robkin Heller felt dangerously close to joining that asphyxiated elite. Mr. Zobiah's instructions washed across his face in oily waves, causing his vision to waver and his olfactory centers to cry out in stunned disbelief. Through the windows he could see the entire student body of Nozzlin High streaming into the afternoon sunshine, leaping jauntily into bullnosed Fords and Mercs, combing their hair, lighting covert cigarettes, hitching their pegged pants, smoothing their tight sweaters. Ah, the jugs. Restrained by bras, they jiggled tightly in place like cantilevered Jell-O. Why had he alone been kept after school to make up lab assignments?

"Heller, please take your hands out of your pockets and pay attention. You're going to be working with sensitive chemicals here, and if you don't perform the operations exactly as I've described them—foof!"

Mr. Zobiah's clever sound effect slid another moist finger of breath into Robkin's nose. Attempting to speak without inhaling, he assured the teacher of his certain ability to perform the experiment flawlessly, even if blindfolded.

Mr. Zobiah was unconvinced, but returned to his desk. Maybe the little putz would lose a finger or something. Sighing, he sank into his swivel seat and lost himself in a recent report on yttrium, soon forgetting Robkin's presence entirely.

Robkin, meanwhile, turned to the racks of chemicals, chose several, and resignedly set to work. As his hands mixed and heated a solution, his mind retreated back to third-period history. In that steamy class he dropped his pencil to the floor an average of twelve times a day in order to bend and sneak quick glances up the tight woolen skirt of Wilma Schmwerper, whose faintly puckered thighs had elevated her to current teen queen of Robkin's beat-off fantasies.

He was *so* horny. If only he could get *laid*. But that mad act seemed virtually unknown in comfy, suburban Nozzlin. Oh, the hood girls probably did it, but the hood girls wore tiny gold crosses around their necks, chewed gum with their mouths open, and mainly were always hanging around with male hoods wearing wide, heavily buckled black belts. Robkin was afraid of the hood girls.

Unfortunately, the sole alternative was the Jewish girls, who wore tiny gold mezuzahs around their necks, chewed gum with their mouths closed, and mainly were always hanging around with their mothers, who laced their food with saltpeter, an Eros nullifier. These circumstances had cut Robkin's options to a bare choice between his left and right hand. There matters stood.

As his mind darted up skirts, through fortresslike girdles into slick, honeyed grottoes, his eyes completely missed the advent of the thick, white vapor that began to pour from the mouth of his test tube. Anticipating perfumed breezes of the delta, he inhaled luxuriously and snorted his lungs full of unknown chemical gas.

The abrupt Verdun of coughing from the lab table launched Mr. Zobiah's journal from his lap like a terrified bird. He glared up, framing a withering epithet, but stopped without speaking. He faced a green-on-green sateen shirt and a pair of black pegged pants, untenanted, doing a small, insane dance before the Bunsen burner. Good lord, he'd hoped for a finger, or even a whole hand, but this was ridiculous. Mumbling formulas, he got rapidly into his overcoat and departed the lab with great dispatch.

Robkin, meanwhile, had controlled his coughing and now stood unmoving, staring at his reflection in the darkening panes of the window. He looked like the Playtex Living Bra commercials, only in Hempstead hood clothes. "Holy shit," he realized, "I'm *invisible*." He stole a glance at the test tube he still held in one hand. Half a tube of silvery liquid remained, winking naughtily at him in the fluorescent lab light. He'd invented an invisibility potion!

The first question that occurred to Robkin's trained Jewish mind was how best to exploit this miracle. Rob a bank and be rich? Infiltrate the Kremlin and steal Russian secrets?

What he really wanted, of course, was to infiltrate a few *vaginas*. But how?

He snapped his fingers suddenly. *The girls' locker room!* If he hurried, he could still catch the showers of the field-hockey team. Scrambling to his feet, he launched himself for the door and, invisibility being a bit tricky to get used to, fell flat on his face amid a clatter of desks and chairs.

The crash was loud and clear out in the hall. Old Walt Bezinski, brooming a ragged line of wine-colored sawdust down the deserted corridor, paused in his work to peer curiously through the door lab. He beheld an empty shirt and pair of pants thrashing wildly amid a small forest of fallen furniture.

"Heh," commented the grizzled prole. Shaking his head wonderingly, he ambled on down the hall.

But Robkin had glimpsed the face at the door. Shmushed against the window glass, it had appeared hostile and ogreish, and had scared him badly before he'd realized who it was. Then he realized something else—he was visible again!

So the potion had a time limit. Some twenty minutes had passed since he first breathed the vapor. Well, twenty minutes would be plenty of time to get him where he was going. Once there, he could take more potion as often as he needed. He turned the test tube to the burner flame and sniffed cautiously about its mouth. Then he removed his clothes.

It took him five minutes to penetrate the still-empty locker room and hide himself inside the mop locker. He'd just wait there until the girls came back—all sweaty and slippery and giggling—recharge his invisibility, and step forth to view the disrobing. And then . . .

The door to the locker flew open, flooding him with light.

"Whuffo you here?" cried Minnie, Nozzlin High's colored cleaning lady, her brown marshmallow arms roiling in indignation. "Whuffo you in the wimmin's locker room? An' *whah is you undress?*"

Shocked, Robkin stared down at himself. He was completely visible and strikingly naked. "Uh, gluck . . ." he said.

"You bess come out of dere 'fore Ah counts five," Minnie warned, "or Ah gwine thruss mah mop in yo' face." She began to count.

Robkin rolled his eyes about wildly. Minnie would march him straight to Mr. Formosa's office, and that would be it for him at Nozzlin High. His parents, Manny and Isobel, would be so scandalized they might have to move to a goyish neighborhood. His palms were sweating so profusely that the test tube nearly slipped from his hand.

Test tube?

"Schmuck!" he realized, smiting his forehead with his other hand, which contained his Zippo windproof lighter and which fetched his left eyebrow a nasty whack. Lighter and test tube. Right. He thrust the former beneath the latter and lit it.

"Fo'! Fi—" Minnie broke off, eyes bulging. "Good hebbins!" she cried. Her feets did their stuff.

Heart still pounding with alarm, Robkin pulled the locker door closed and sank down upon a bucket. Holy shit. And why had the potion worn off so soon? Had he inhaled too little? Or was the reversibility triggered by something other than passage of time? Abruptly he realized that both times he'd been scared. First Walt had scared him, and then Minnie, and each time he'd popped into visibility like a pudgy light bulb.

Fear made him visible.

But . . . holy shit! How could he invisibly fondle and finger in the girls' locker room when the main thing he *feared* was girls? Maybe he ought to forget the whole thing, go back to the lab for his clothes, and see if he couldn't find Steamin' or Mr. Rock 'n' Roll and listen to some records or something. Yeah, shit. He stood up and reached for the door.

SHRIEK! CRASH! GIGGLE!

Robkin yanked his hand from the door as if it were red hot and shrank against the rear wall of the locker. Too late! The girls had returned. He doubted if he could even walk through them without being scared enough to turn visible. Look at him now, for God's sake. Even inside the locker he'd turned visible. He'd have to wait them out, stay right where he was until they'd all left.

Suddenly, he heard the voice of Mrs. Butch, the large-shouldered girls' gym teacher, seeming very close. "Carlotta, Leonia, I don't know where Minnie is today, but this room hasn't been mopped. After you finish your showers, I'd like you two to do it. You'll find mops and buckets right in here."

WHANG, WHANG, WHANG went her fist against the locker wall next to Robkin's right ear. Good Christ! he thought.

"Miz Butch? How come *Ah* always is de one dat has to do de moppin' an' stuff?" said a voice Robkin recognized as Carlotta ("San Juan") Hilton. "How come Ah nebber gets to go to de office wif de attendance, like de white an' de Jewish girls?"

"Thass right," agreed a second voice. "It not because we member of a mah-nority group, is it?"

"You're both quite sweaty," said Mrs. Butch's voice. "Take your showers." Sharp footsteps receded.

"Fuckin' jive bitch," muttered the Carlotta voice, fading off into the generalized locker-room babble of squeals, gossip, and giggles.

Robkin whimpered softly to himself. Obviously, he had to do something before they came for the mops. He'd better calm himself, collect his thoughts. Slowly, the pounding in his chest subsided. Well, he'd just have to screw up his courage and use his invisibility to get himself out of there. After all, invisibility *was* something no teen-ager in the world had ever possessed before. Feeling cool and controlled, he made himself invisible and eased from the locker.

One glance shattered his control instantly. His hands and feet began to shimmer into substance. With a cry, he hurled himself back inside the locker and pulled the door closed just in time. Good God, the room had been filled with naked women! He had seen bush! How was he supposed *not* to be scared when there was pubic hair all over the place?

He glanced at his test tube. There was enough potion left for a single dose, no more. Well, he really didn't have a choice. He'd have to squeeze his eyes nearly shut and make a run for it. Emerging from the locker, he took six steps, turned a corner into one of the locker alcoves, and found himself face to face with Wilma Schmwerper. Wilma was removing her bra.

His fear abruptly forgotten, Robkin decided to stick around and watch for a while.

Wilma, after all, had filled his every masturbatory fantasy since he'd been seated in front of her last September. Her lips were full and Semitic; her eyes round, dark, and dumb. And . . . *good God, what a pair of knockers!* She'd just finally gotten the third hook of her bra undone, and the underthing had practically exploded off her. She was like the women in the magazines! Almost unbidden, his hand reached out for her.

"Hey, Wilma," bawled a voice, "Ah show you mah hickey?"

"Why, no, Carlotta, you didn't."

"Well, den feas' yo' eyes on *dis*."

Carlotta, nude and very black, passed within inches of

144

Robkin to sit beside Wilma on the low wooden bench. She indicated a discolored spot on her neck. With a small coo of admiration, Wilma bent to look; and one of her soft, pink and white breasts lightly nudged one of Carlotta's firm black ones. The girls' eyes locked for an electric instant. Carlotta licked her lips.

"I wonder if the showers are ready?" Wilma asked, a little breathlessly.

"Ah sho' hopes so," said Carlotta. "Ah is *ready*." She took Wilma's hand, and the two of them padded away, glancing at each other with shy excitement.

Robkin was stunned. Things like this went on? In the girls' locker room? While the boys hid in lonely toilet stalls, pulling their miserable wires and dreaming of better days? Holy shit! But, then, he'd always somehow known that this was what happened in girls' locker rooms. He hadn't *believed* it, but he'd known it.

Wow.

But this was no time for philosophizing. By now, most of the girls had passed his alcove, towels over their arms, bosoms all ashiver. He'd just bring up the rear, as it were. Squaring his shoulders, he fell in behind Carolyn Czezarski, a girl who took home ec and typing classes, and followed her fat little tushie all the way to the shower room.

The entrance way billowed steam, hiding the interior, but he could hear many showers and, above them, coos, whimpers, and moans. God, the guys would *never* believe this.

Carolyn hung her towel on a peg and sidled into the steam. Swallowing, Robkin followed.

At first he could see nothing. Then like an airplane emerging suddenly from a cloud, he could see *everything*. All about him were girls—girls he'd been passing in the halls and sitting next to for years—utterly naked, stroking and fondling and sliding against one another, their matted woollies like small, drowned mammals. The whole room seemed perfumed with . . . well, an odor much like low tide at Coney Island. But good! He was immersed in a steaming chowder of slick flesh and sweet, funky broth. Checking with his hand, he found that he'd gotten the boner of a lifetime.

But what should he *do*? He felt like a small child set free in the world's greatest candy store. He wanted *everything*.

He decided to start with an appetizer. He would squeeze the small, rodentlike bosoms of Darlene Dell'Olio. He stepped over to her, reached out a hand . . . and began to feel afraid. With alarm, he saw his hands, feet, and German helmet blink into view. Good God. He stepped back, closed his eyes, and concentrated with all his might on not being scared, on not feeling anything. Taking a breath, he opened his eyes and looked. His extremities were invisible again. He sighed with relief.

But when he reached with his hand, he found that his hard-on was gone.

Fighting a terrible, sinking feeling, he gave himself a new hard-on and reached for Carolyn . . . and felt frightened and began to turn visible. He stepped back and dampened his emotions . . . and stayed invisible . . . but lost his hard-on.

Gritting his teeth, he made one more stab. He reached for Wilma Schmwerper . . . and began to feel afraid.

"Ah, shit!" he yelled so loudly that several nearby girls turned to stare.

But, of course, they saw nothing.

Two Cock Tales

I

The telephone rang, loud as a fire alarm. To Bernie Boom-Boom, snoozing stoned on the sofa, his mind drifting off through Middle Earth somewhere, the sound was like twin jets of ice water shot in his ears.

"O.K., fuck you, I'm coming!" Bernie shook his head to clear it, which was the approximate equivalent of shaking a jar of muddy water in order to see better through it, and stood up. On its fourth ring, Bernie reached the phone and put his hand on the receiver. Then he paused. There were a number of persons, mostly individuals to whom he owed money, with whom it would make little sense to speak. On the other hand, his caller just might be someone who owed *him* money, or better yet, one of his girl friends wanting to come over and sit on his face. What to do, what to do. As the phone initiated its seventh ring, Bernie lifted the receiver and said hello.

"Hello, is this Mr. Boom-Boom?" Well, the voice was female and very sexy. Surprise!

"Why, yes, this is Mr. Boom-Boom," said Bernie, wagging his eyebrows roguishly. "What can I do for you?"

"Well, this is Miss Morgan, Mr. Boom-Boom. From the telephone company?"

Bernie's rakish smile inverted. Shit.

"Uh, I suppose this is about my bill?" Of his many creditors, the telephone company had been the most predatory. For the last month, a certain Mr. DeReimer had been calling him every other day, first asking, then importuning, finally demanding that his bill be paid. Of late, a strange paranoia-inducing tone had entered the man's voice and Bernie had sensed veiled threats. Well, at least a woman's voice would be an improvement.

"Yes, I'm afraid it is about your bill. I hate to harass you in your home, Mr. Boom-Boom, but it's my job to remind you. You're four months overdue, you know."

"I know, I know," said Bernie. "You people never let me forget for long. What happened to Mr. DeReimer, by the way?"

"Oh, he's been transferred to Corporate Accounts. I think the company decided he was a little ... strident, and that they could catch more flies with sugar than with vinegar." She paused. "Uh, I hope you don't take that to mean I think of you as a fly, Mr. Boom-Boom."

Bernie laughed. He kind of liked this Miss Morgan. Maybe he could bullshit her. "No, I don't take it that way. I know you have your job to do. You see, here's the problem: I'm a musician in a group and these two record companies are suing each other to find out which owns us and in the meantime all our money is frozen. But they'll be settling it within a week or two and then I'll be mailing in the entire amount I owe you. So do you suppose you could carry me for just a couple more weeks? Please?"

"A group? Really? Which one?" Miss Morgan suddenly sounded extremely interested.

"Why, uh, the Scumbags. You know, we're one of those . . ."

"*The Scumbags??* I love the Scumbags! I see you all the *time* at the Mercer Center for Bisexual Decadence of the Forties! Which one are you, Mr. Boom-Boom?"

This was working even better than he'd expected. Miss Morgan seemed to have forgotten all about his bill. He'd have to remember this musician bit, use it again sometime. "Which one am I? Why, I'm the ... bass player."

"The *bass* player? That's incredible! Do you know how many nights I've stood almost next to you, just staring? But I thought your name was Johnny Farts. . . ."

"Oh, right, Johnny Farts. That's my *stage* name. I mean, how would it sound if they announced 'On bass, Bernie Boom-Boom?' That's not decadent at all. Besides, it sounds like a drummer's name."

Miss Morgan giggled. "Wow," she said, "I can't believe I'm talking to you. All my friends think you're the sexiest Scumbag of all."

"Heh heh," said Bernie. "And what about you? What do *you* think?"

"Me? God, I think you're the sexiest man I've ever seen!"

"Really? That's what you think?"

"Oh, yes. All that long blond hair and . . ."

"And what?"

"Mr. Boom-Boom, I just realized. I shouldn't be talking to you like this. I mean, I called to . . ."

"Call me Bernie. And what?"

Her voice dropped an octave, became soft and flirtatious. "And that big lump in your pants."

"In my . . ."

"Mmmm, yes, that's why I stand so close to you when you play. So I can see it thrust against your jeans when you move your hips."

Bernie glanced down into his lap. She was right, there *was* a big lump in his pants. And she was giving it to him. He wondered suddenly what time she got off work. "Uh, Miss Morgan, I wonder if . . ."

"Call me Mitzi. You know what I think about when I see it, Bernie?"

"No. No, I don't, Mitzi. What do you think about?"

"I think about sucking it. I think about running my tongue all up and down it while I'm tickling your balls with my fingernails."

Oh . . . yeah? He certainly hadn't been expecting anything like this when he'd answered the phone. His erection was threatening to burst his fly. He adjusted it to a more comfortable position and licked his lips.

"Uh, Mitzi, maybe we could get together tonight. And, you know . . ."

There was a long pause. Was he going too fast? Had he blown it?

"Bernie?"

"Yeah?"

"We don't have to wait until tonight."

"You mean you can come over now?"

"No, I mean . . . unscrew the earpiece of your phone."

"Unscrew the . . ."

"The earpiece of your phone. You know, that circular piece of black plastic you hear my voice coming from?"

"But I don't . . ."

"Bernie, just do it. Trust me."

"Uh, O.K. Hold on." He took the receiver from his ear and, with some difficulty, began unscrewing the earpiece. After several turns, it came loose in his hand. He caught his breath sharply. Inside the earpiece was a mouth!

Bernie blinked his eyes several times and shook his head, but when he looked again, the mouth was still there. Or rather a pair of lips, faintly lipsticked and beestung, in the *Penthouse* manner. He tried to say something but the words choked off in his throat.

Then the lips smiled, and a glistening pink tongue emerged to lick them wetly.

"Yah!" cried Bernie, and dropped the receiver on the floor.

"Pick me up! Pick me up!" called the phone.

Bernie hastened to do so. Holding the receiver gingerly between thumb and forefinger, he stared into the earpiece and tried to think of something to say.

"What kind of shit is that," demanded the lips, "dropping me before you even get to know me? Maybe you'd like to get back to your phone bill."

"No, no, no," assured Barnie. "I'm sorry. You startled me. I didn't expect . . ."

"Well, it's O.K.," said the lips, mollified. "No harm done. Except . . . I'd feel a lot better if you held me more tightly."

Swallowing, Bernie wrapped his fingers around the receiver. It felt strangely warm against his skin.

"Mmmmm," said the phone. "Now hold me closer."

"Uh . . ." said Bernie. He slowly brought the receiver back against the side of his face.

"That's the idea," said the lips, softly brushing his earlobe. "Now, how do you like <u>this</u>?" And Bernie felt the tongue slide wetly into his ear.

"Yah!" he cried again. He ripped the phone from his face and a long strand of saliva sagged like a jump rope between him and the earpiece.

"Don't drop me! Don't drop me!" piped the phone.

"I won't drop you," said Bernie. "It's just that you keep taking me by surprise. Actually, that felt very nice."

The lips smiled. "Want to feel something nicer?"

"Uh, sure," said Bernie.

"Then kiss me." The lips puckered expectantly.

Good Lord! Well, he'd done weirder things in his time. Although he couldn't think of any of them right now. Gathering the receiver in both hands, he brought the earpiece to his mouth and pressed the lips tentatively against his.

The lips responded, shyly at first, then with growing passion. Bernie had never experienced a kiss quite like it. Then the tongue entered his mouth like a sweet, hot fish, and his sense of shock at the circumstances began rapidly to segue into lust. Finally, he pulled the receiver away. "Wow," he murmured. "Listen, let's get high."

"Good," said the lips, panting lightly. "But hurry."

Bernie placed the receiver in his lap and began rolling a joint. He couldn't remember when he'd felt so turned on. Hurriedly, he licked the number closed, lit it, and thrust the j into the earpiece.

The phone took a long toke and held its breath. So did Bernie. After four or five such hits each, he laid the roach in the ashtray.

"Kiss me hard," said the phone.

Bernie didn't have to be told twice. He pushed the earpiece against his mouth and kissed the lips hard.

"Mmmmm," they said. The phone cord began to spiral around his thigh, snaking sensuously against him. "Feel me, feel me good," begged the lips.

Feel her? Feel what? With a mental shrug of the shoulders, Bernie placed the body of the phone in his lap and began to caress it.

"Ohhhhhhhhh," said the lips.

Then Bernie's hand moved through the cradle and his fingers brushed one of the plastic hang-up bottons.

"OHHHHHHHHHH," said the lips.

Oh, really? He went back to the button, took it between thumb and forefinger, and rolled it in small, oscillating circles.

"OHHHHHHHHHHHHHHHHHHH," said the lips. "OH, MY GOD!"

Bernie jerked his hand away. Had he hurt her?

"God, I just came," said the lips. "You've got me hearing beeper tones. What was *in* that dope?" The phone sighed happily. "But then you rock stars always get the best dope."

"Rock stars?" The dope had also done a number on Bernie's head. "Oh, right, rock stars. Got the biggest cocks, too," he said casually.

"I don't believe you," the phone teased. "Show me."

"Show you? You can see?"

"No, but I think I can estimate pretty well . . . with my mouth."

"Oh . . . yeah?" said Bernie, and before he'd finished the "yeah," his pants were down to his knees and his cock was jutting from his lap like a starved stork straining for food. "Estimate away," he told the phone and brought the ear well of the receiver slowly over the head of his cock. The lips shmwerped out to meet him, then sucked him in.

"Glmph!" said the phone, and its tongue began to describe rapid circles around Bernie's German helmet. It felt as if he'd stuck himself into the center of a spinning car-wash brush made from liver. The sensation was so intense it was almost unbearable. In fact, it *was* unbearable, all tease with none of that cross-shaft massage so vital to coming. He tried to jam himself further into the receiver.

"MMLKPT! STPPM!" screamed the phone. Startled, Bernie pulled the receiver clear. "Nine one one! Nine one one!" the lips cried. "Police, fire, emergency!"

"Hey, shush," said Bernie. "I'm sorry. I got carried away. You were driving me crazy."

"Who do you think I am, Linda Lovelace?" demanded the phone. "You can *see* how skinny my neck is."

"I said I was sorry. Listen, I've got to fuck you." Bernie's balls were throbbing like small hearts. "You've got to come over here right away." He gave one of her hang-up buttons a twist to place emphasis on his request.

"Anh! Anh!" responded the lips. "God, yes. I want to fuck you too, Bernie. And I don't have to come over. Unscrew my baseplate. Hurry!"

This time Bernie asked no questions. He took the body of the phone from his lap and turned it upside down. The baseplate was held in place by two small screws. Bernie went to work with his fingernail.

"Hurry," said the phone. "Please hurry." Thick, funky juices were beginning to ooze from several small holes in the baseplate to make hot trails on Bernie's wrist. The first screw came loose and he moved to the second. He felt clumsy as a schoolboy dealing with his first bra clasps. His fingernail broke, so he switched fingers. At last the screw pulled free and the baseplate fell away.

An Afro of pubic hair burst forth, and great clouds of fishy perfume. Bernie blinked and pulled the phone closer. Deep within the hair, almost lost in it, pink labia twinkled.

"Fuck me!" cried the phone. "Oh, fuck me, fuck me!"

In a steamy frenzy, Bernie propped the receiver upside down between his head and neck, so that he could kiss the lips. With his other hand he slid the phone slowly over his dong, well over it, all the way down. It felt incredible. He groaned and began moving himself slowly in and out, in and out, in . . .

There was a click.

The lips went dead beneath his, dead as plastic. A small, mechanical whine started from the body of the phone. Bernie fired his glance to his groin, just in time to witness the metal claw device complete its encirclement of his swollen balls.

"Now, then, Mr. Boom-Boom," said Mr. DeReimer, "about that overdue bill . . ."

II

Wilbur the Wimp thought of his cock as a pressure valve.

That is, when Wilbur felt tension accumulating as a foreshadow of some upcoming event, he would vent his anxiety by masturbating. If, say, he had to make a crucial presentation to senior executives at the office, he would dash wildly into the men's room a short time before and flail away in a toilet stall, only to emerge moments later the very picture of coolness and self-possession. When it was up to him to captain his two-man badminton team to victory at the local Y, he would feel more and more uptight all afternoon until finally, just before the game, he would beat off into a handkerchief in the rear of the locker room and then stride manfully onto the court. Thus it was that when he finally obtained a date with Jug-City Sharon, the incredibly desirable bartender at Dr. Depravity's, and had by seven o'clock become so uptight that his intestines felt tied in a knot, he naturally assumed that the thing to do was beat the meat.

Since Sharon didn't get off work until eight, there was no need to rush things, to employ the simple zip-jerk techniques he was forced to use in public places. So what would it be tonight? The liver and vibrators? The electric plastic vagina he had mail-ordered from Amsterdam? No, wait, he had it: the vacuum cleaner! He hadn't used the vacuum cleaner in at least two weeks. Not only did it do the job slowly and well, it also disposed of the consequences without the need for Kleenex or towels. The vacuum would be the very thing.

So he went to the closet where he kept his brooms and mops and floor wax, removed the vacuum cleaner, and carried it into the living room. It consisted of a squat canister on wheels and a flexible hose of accordioned plastic, some six feet in length. The all-purpose rug-floor nozzle he removed and set aside.

He plugged the machine into the wall and himself into the soft ruberoid hose end. Taking a seat on the sofa, he closed his eyes and nudged the kick switch with his toe. The vacuum cleaner roared to life and his flaccid dong began to fibrillate furiously in the hose, making a loud fart noise. Quickly, though, his member became hard and the fart noise turned high-pitched, like the noise made by kids blowing through empty Good & Plenty boxes. The cozy hose (or, if you prefer, the hosey cooz) snuggled and tore at him. He began to fantasize, imagining Jug-City Sharon in place of the vacuum, watching her breasts orbit the axis of her chest like twin Comet Kohouteks, only unlit. And much bigger. Oh, it was being a wonderful beat-off!

Then the vacuum cleaner made a loud coughing sound and, with a *blam*, blew off its lid. Wilbur snapped his eyes open. The exposed motor was belching brown smoke, through which red flames licked. What was more, his cock was being sucked with ever-increasing force, deeper and deeper into the hose. *Good Lord,* thought Wilbur, *I better ditch!* He kicked the switch with his foot. Nothing happened! If he didn't act fast, he'd be able to get a job guarding a harem. Launching himself from the sofa, he tore the electric cord free of the wall. The motor stopped abruptly and, with it, the seven-hundred-mile-an-hour winds that were occurring within the hose. *Whew,* thought Wilbur. *Crackle crackle,* went the flames. *Whoops,* thought Wilber. He ran for the bathroom, dragging hose and canister bumpily after him.

Flinging the shower curtain aisde, he spun knobs until the water was going full blast, then dumped the canister into the tub. Emitting a mighty hiss and a cloud of vile-smelling smoke, the vacuum cleaner died.

God, thought Wilbur. He turned the water off and headed for the window to air out the room. There was a heavy tug at his groin. The hose and he were still engaged! In his rush to douse the flames, he'd forgotten all about that aspect of things. He reached down, took the hose in both hands, and attempted to pull it away from his body.

The hose would not pull.

What? thought Wilbur. He pulled again, harder. "Ouch!" he cried. This was ridiculous. How could he be stuck? He'd vacuumed off half a hundred times and never gotten stuck before. Then again, he'd never experienced the jet-stream effect before either. There was no doubt about it, though; he and the hose were stuck tight. To complicate matters, he still had a large hard-on and the hose end was acting like one of those brass cock rings that were rumored to be used by Japanese to maintain night-long erections. His only hope for freedom was to finish beating himself off.

He detached himself from the canister, went back to the living room, and tried an experimental beat or two. But the hose, engineered not to collapse under conditions of severe suction, wouldn't give beneath his hand and he couldn't feel a thing. What was he going to do? He checked out the time. Seven-thirty. He began to panic. Maybe if he unbent a coat hanger and stuck it down the far end . . . no, that was stupid. Well, suppose he poured cold water into . . . no, that was stupider. But he had to do something. It might be months before Jug-City Sharon could find another open night to bestow on him.

Maybe he should just show up with the hose slung over his shoulder. He could explain that he was just coming from a costume party, to which he had gone as a gas pump. He wouldn't actually have to *give* gas, due to the shortages, and . . . no, no, no, what was he thinking? He must be getting hysterical. No, the only thing to do was somehow hide the whole thing under his clothes.

So Wilbur took the hose and coiled it around and around itself until he had created a tight plastic spiral around the central point of his groin. But as soon as he let it go, it unwound violently, its metal coupling end almost slugging him in the jaw. He'd have to hold it in place somehow. He rewound the spiral and this time bound it securely to his body with long strips of masking tape.

Now to dress. Underpants were out, obviously. It would take a pair of drawers designed for Haystack Calhoun to contain both him and the coil. In fact, how was he going to get into any of his pants? Then he remembered the old pair of trousers his father had given him once, as a sarcastic comment on the tightness of his son's jeans. It was not that his father had been fat but that the trousers were thirty years old and thus had pleats that mattered. He found them at the bottom of his old clothes drawer and crossing his fingers, stepped into them. They fit! The waist was just high enough and the pleats just sufficiently stretchable to cover both him and the hose.

He checked himself out in the mirror. He looked pregnant! He couldn't take out Jug-City Sharon looking *pregnant*. He began tearing through his dresser, hurling clothes in all directions, searching for something, anything, that would cover his unsightly bulge. At last he understood why all those copies of *Weight Watchers* were sold each month.

Wait, the sweater. The baggy old sweater he'd bought in the antique shop. He pulled it over his head, down over his hips, and went again to the mirror. He looked . . . passable. Not gorgeous, but passable. Well . . . he glanced at the clock. Ten of. Jesus Christ. He darted back to the bathroom and scrutinized his face. No ripe zits, nothing stuck between his teeth, but his hair . . . his normally full, curly head of hair was still soaking wet from the shower!

Wilbur grabbed a towel and dried his hair as best he could. Then he combed it. He didn't much like the way it looked, all slicked back against his head, but it was an improvement. As a matter of fact, he didn't like the way *any* of him looked. He felt ridiculous, like a character from some old movie. *Why tonight, God.* Wilbur implored.

Bong bong bong . . . went the clock.

Uh-oh, thought Wilbur, and headed out the door. Jug-City Sharon didn't like to be kept waiting.

It was a warm spring night and Dr. Depravity's, the singles bar across the street from his apartment building, was filled to overflowing. The best thing to do would be to get her out of there and into a dark movie house where nobody could see him. Already he was attracting stares. He pushed through the milling crowd on the street, into the entrance. A large, red-faced man guarded the inner door with a cashbox and a fluorescent wrist stamp.

"Uh, I'm not staying," Wilbur told him. "I'm just here to pick up Sharon."

"Who are you supposed to be?" the man demanded. "Scott Fitzgerald?" He laughed coarsely and slapped his thigh.

"Hey, fuck you," said Wilbur. "Do you think I *want* to be . . ."

"Hi, Wilbur," called a bright voice. Jug-City Sharon was just stepping through the inner door. Wilbur felt his knees grow weak. She looked incredible. Her waist was bare and her very tight, very white pants contrasted shockingly with the tan of her tummy. Her hair cascaded to her shoulders like an ebon waterfall; her moist, full, slightly parted lips were a blatant invitation to unknown, juicy places. And, most spectacular of all, encased in a halter that was like fat, burnt-orange spiderwebs, were Sharon's breasts.

Overripe is not the word. They strained and swung and

danced like great fleshy hornets' nests. If they had been army water bags, she could have sustained a platoon in a desert for a week. And tonight, they just might be his to fondle and bounce and get lost in. Wilbur swallowed, his Adam's apple feeling large as a movie hillbilly's.

"Gee, Wilbur," said Sharon, "you look weird tonight. What's with your hair?"

"He t'inks he's Scott Fitzgerald," said the red-faced man, and roared anew, holding his belly with both hands.

"Why, you *do* look like Scott Fitzgerald," cried Sharon. "Oh, Wilbur, I had no idea you were so *now*." And she walked up to him and gave him a big kiss on the lips.

"Oh, well, heh heh," said Wilbur.

"Hrmph," said the red-faced man. He vanished behind his *Daily News*.

"Gosh, Wilbur, I was sort of thinking we'd go to the movies tonight, but you look so fantastic we should go over to Sodom & Gomorrah instead, just to show you off."

"Oh, uh, Sodom & Gomorrah? Funny, I was thinking about a movie too." Sodom & Gomorrah was one of those new, decadent night spots that were springing up around town. The chic-est, trendiest, most intimidating people in the city went there to dance and strut about for one another. It was the last place in the world Wilbur would have chosen to go, especially tonight.

"Come on, Wilbur," said Sharon. "You can always go to a movie, but you hardly ever look the way you do tonight."

"Well, that's true. But that's exactly why I . . ."

"Then let's go." She pulled Wilbur through the door and flagged down a cab.

In the warm back seat, Sharon cuddled close to him and began planting small kisses along the line of his jaw. *Wow*, thought Wilbur, and began kissing back. Her lips were fantastic. *She* was fantastic. It was as if one of his adolescent fantasy women had come to life. She put her hand on his leg and began moving it groinward . . . and suddenly he felt his cock straining against the firm, ridged walls of the vacuum hose, and masking tape beginning to tear. On the verge of panic, he reached down and gently pushed her hand away.

She gave him a disbelieving look.

"Not now," Wilbur improvised, "I'll, uh, be embarrassed to stand up."

"But they *like* it at Sodom & Gomorrah when you walk in with an obvious hard-on. It's *stylish*."

Wilbur thought fast. "Listen, uh, the people who go to this place . . . you wouldn't describe them as a Republican crowd, would you?"

"What? No, of course not."

"Then it wouldn't be so hip for me to go as an elephant, would it?"

Sharon chuckled throatily and regarded him through lowered lashes. "No, I guess it wouldn't. Well, we'll check out your . . . trunk later." She curled up under his arm, dropped a couple of downs, and looked out a window.

Shortly thereafter, Wilbur and Sharon were walking arm in arm into Sodom & Gomorrah. A wall of deafening music engulfed them.

"Ooh, they're playing 'Dead Battery Vibrator Blues,'" squealed Sharon. "Let's dance!"

"Uh, gee, I was thinking maybe a beer."

"Come on, Wilbur, you can have a beer later." She dragged him through the crowd of men in ballet tutus, women smoking cigars, and other individuals of moot gender with glitter and purple iridescent hair. By the time they reached the dance floor, the band was just beginning a new number, a ballad called "Killing Me Softly with His Knife."

"Mmmm," observed Sharon, "a slow one." She fit herself into Wilbur's arms and placed her cheek against his. They began to shuffle in small squares. To his acute chagrin, Sharon immediately attempted to grind her hips against him. In an insane, reverse parody of all those high-school slow dances during which the girls eschewed groin contact, Wilbur found himself dancing with his ass humped back in the air.

"Don't be unfriendly," scolded Sharon. She encircled his waist with her arms and pulled his hips against her. Groin met hose coil and she bounced away again.

Sharon stared at him with sudden new respect. "Wilbur, wow, I didn't realize—I mean, if I'd known." She pushed her hips back against him, more gently this time. "Oh, my God, Wilbur," she breathed, and held him very tight.

"Heh heh," said Wilbur.

He was feeling increasingly nervous. To get his mind off his dilemma, he began to look at the people around them. It was at this point that he first noticed the looks they were giving him.

"Pretty tacky Fitzgerald," sniffed a haughty blonde in Thirties clothes and Joan Crawford fuck-me shoes.

"Yeah," agreed her partner, who was wearing a double-breasted Clark Gable suit and spats. "Who's that little creep think he is, being so lame in front of us?"

Wilbur swallowed, feeling more uptight than ever. These decadence people were even more intimidating than he'd expected. *Yeesh,* he thought, and buried his face in Sharon's hair.

After a time, the band brought the ballad to a ragged close and launched into their current hit single, "Coal Chute Boogie (Kaka on My Wah-Wah)."

"Hey, a fast one!" cried Sharon. "C'mon, Wilbur, get it on!" And she began to shake and shimmy like a Jell-O person in an earthquake.

Oy vey, thought Wilbur in English. More of the masking tape was pulling loose every minute. He began to dance solely from the waist up, sort of a reverse Bo Diddley.

All around them, people were leaving off their own dancing to glom the mad dervish of Jug-City Sharon. Soon a circle had cleared with them at the center. Then some schmuck turned a spotlight on them.

"God, look at the way the creep *with* her is dancing," said a very skinny woman with Deco dress and Deco hairdo.

"Where'd *he* learn to dance?" asked a gesticulating gay in a nun's habit. "At a school for spastics?"

"I resent that," said a spastic.

Wilbur's eyes were blazing. Damn it, he was a good dancer. He'd show them. "Whoo!" he yelled, and executed a split in the James Brown manner.

"Attaboy, Wilbur," called Sharon.

Encouraged, Wilbur pulled out the stops. No *Soul Train* regular had ever looked badder. The withering comments ceased and the crowd drew back in new respect.

"Wilbur, you're fantastic!" Sharon glided close to him, shimmying her breasts like coconuts in a hurricane. In sudden dip, she went down on one knee before him and unzipped his fly.

With a loud *sproing* and a tearing of tape, Wilbur's hose burst forth and flew across the room. It looked like the spring snake from a trick can of nuts.

Oh, no, thought Wilbur, *no, no!* He wished he would die, disappear, never have been born. Now he'd never get to snuggle Sharon's shelf. Shit, she'd probably never want to see him again.

The band broke off. Every eye in the room was on him. The silence was deafening. Then . . .

"That's the most decadent thing I've ever seen," exclaimed a fat, bearded black in a little girl's dress.

"*Incredibly* decadent," agreed a quadruple amputee on a wooden cart.

To Wilbur's amazement, the band now struck up "For He's a Degenerate Fellow," a number they usually reserved for the entrance of, say, a David Bowie or a Richard Speck. The crowd swirled around him, congratulating him and pounding him on the back.

"Oh, Wilbur," cried Sharon, throwing her arms around him. "My hero!"

"Oh, well," said Wilbur. "Hey hey."

And for the next eight hours, they lived happily ever after.

The Way to Become
the Masculine He-man

Yes, even you can become a masculine he-man. You don't have to be a football hero or get into fights at tough bars. The amount of hair on your chest is irrelevant. You can even have a sensitive mind. Shit, I got a sensitive mind.

Masculinity is measured one way and one way only—by how well you make love. In a nut cup, that is what you will learn reading this essay.

For the last five years, women have been calling me Casanova, Valentino, a hunk, my proud telephone pole, liver lips (in the most flattering Afro-American sense), and that perfect combination of herbivore in the living room and wild stud Chevrolet out in the garage.

Some of the most interesting women in America have fallen in love with me—a cough-drop heiress, a celebrated popularizer of centipedes, a topless anesthetist, Annie the Witch, and, this week, two of the Plaster Casters of Chicago. On a recent cross-country flight, I fulfilled a lifelong dream by making love standing up with a stewardess in a locked toilet compartment at forty thousand feet.

In New York, three meter maids, overcome with my masculine aura, shouldered me into a Laundromat and had their way with me. For a laugh, I thawed a frigid jet-setter (you'd recognize her name the minute I mentioned it!), and today she is happily married to a wealthy Jew and has three station wagons.

Yet you'd never believe all this from looking at me. I'm not particularly handsome or rugged. My ears are too big, my nasal hair hangs out, and I have only one nipple. My breath can strip paint. I suffer from frequent public epileptic seizures and must carry a spoon prominently in my breast pocket for bystanders to thrust between my tongue and teeth.

I am not brilliant, nor do I have a magnetic personality. In fact, I am rather stupid and vile.

Husbands and male friends think of me as that smelly kid they used to avoid in the locker room. I'm sure they believe I never "get any," if they think about it at all. But while you husbands and male friends are jealously regarding that fantastic-looking novelist/tiger-hunter with the disquieting bulge in his jodhpurs, *I'm* the one who's off in the linen closet, diving into your wife's pudding.

For, through hard work and a lot of lust, I have become a masculine he-man.

Which is what every woman wants.

More than good looks.

More than brains.

More than money.

More than peace at last and rice for all the people.

Men who can hold a job, cut a dashing figure, or buy her furs are a dime a dozen compared to the man who can skillfully excite the underhang of her buttock with a Water-Pik, and you can learn thousands of irresistible tricks like that right here!

Even if you're ugly, mean, and creepy, even if you're so covered with running sores that you have to sleep in a crib to keep from sliding out of bed, you can learn to make her feel her special uniqueness as a sexual object. For the how-tos of all this basically dirty behavior, just keep reading.

1. Sex—Jeez, It's Terrific

I used to masturbate watching the weather lady. Having tasted the delights of real flesh-and-blood women for five years now, I think I can safely say that the weather lady was better.

Nonetheless, real women are terrific. Especially now. The pill allows you to have all the fun you want with no responsibility whatsoever. And good loving relaxes your muscles, clears up your eczema, takes your mind off the bombing, and puts you in touch with the Krishna.

You say you're not sure you can do it? You say your wazoo hasn't surpassed the stiffness of week-old celery since your grandmother caught you playing with it when you were thirteen?

Relax.

I changed my flaccid ways and so can you. I used to be such a loser you wouldn't believe it. My every attempt at initiating conversation with a woman would cause my tongue to swell like decomposing liver, rendering me incapable of intelligible speech. Then my nose would droop long taffies into my lungs so that I hawked and spit uncontrollably until my intended conquest stumbled away, gagging. So I stayed home nights, crocheting.

I knew that inside I was seething with passion, rather like a refrigerator with a fire inside and the door closed. I knew that if I didn't let my emotions surface they would burn my chives and explode my Seven-Up. Outside, my decorator colors might glow with health and a good sponging, but inside—the pathos of a burst bulb, the semantic anxiety of charred chard. What would I do?

I wish I could tell you that my revelation of how to become a masculine he-man came to me while watching *Junior Frolics*, sniffing bay rum, or carrying that weight, but actually it leaped to mind while I was scrubbing smegma from a cabbage.

Within six months, I was attracting women's stares on the street. Within another six, the stares had turned to loud verbal abuse. However, six months after that, I decided I had graduated. Nowadays, even my lunch hours are booked up months in advance. Women bums rush up to wipe my windshield and stay for their first decent mouthful of protein in years. Last week, my aunt's normally sedate St. Bernard held me in a corner, snarling and baring her teeth, until I consented to be her back-door man. Supermarket check-out girls have begun slipping their panties into my grocery bag for me to find when I got home. Attractive receptionists ignore my announcements of appointments, offering instead a special conference with Mary Palm and her five daughters.

But let me tell you some case histories, lest you think my breakthrough was a fluke and won't work for you.

My friend Murray confessed to me one evening that he was thirty-seven years old, had been married twice, currently had a lover, and still hadn't had a single erection in his life. I told him my secret sex program, and two weeks later, in a bus-terminal men's room, a gay youth whispered a whimsical suggestion and Murray's sudden erection cracked the porcelain of his urinal! Not bad, Murray!

Then there was Louis. Louis had a clubthumb, a sunken chest, and a face like a runny pizza. He was also very self-conscious. He had convinced himself that he was too sticky-looking for interpersonal sex and sought solace in the printed page, spending his nights at home scrutinizing split-beaver magazines.

Then I explained my Masculinity Course. Louis was doubtful, but had nothing to lose. Drawing out his life's savings, he wangled a leave of absence from his job and took his vacation that year on a remote Pacific atoll inhabited solely by lepers.

At last, Louis felt secure. He had his first sexual experience—and loved it! He spent the rest of the summer learning every way he could please a woman sexually. By skillfully mixing his partners, he was able to familiarize himself with the entire female body, and at summer's end, he returned home to Ohio. Though outwardly he looked about the same, there was a strange new masculine aura about him. Women who had previously retched at his presence were suddenly interested. Eventually, a waitress accepted his invitation to go out, and Louis' newly acquired sexual prowess drove her insane. Naturally, he wanted to see her again, but they wouldn't let her out. So Louis met another girl. She, too, sensed that special new aura about him. They had dinner together and discovered that they both loved pistachio ice cream, Alfred Hitchcock movies, and fungus. Louis took her home and they made love. Soon after, they were married.

Ironically, a month after the wedding, Louis' special new aura was diagnosed as leprosy and he was deported.

But down to business.

2. Becoming Masculine

How exactly are you supposed to accomplish these miracles? There are four keys to masculinity:

1. C sharp
2. F
3. D
4. A flat.

Memorize them.

Next, your body. Your body is your guitar. If it is beat up and out of tune, you're not going to get played by Bo Diddley. So we might as well turn you into a Gibson guy with these masculinity exercises:

MASCULINITY EXERCISE NUMBER 1   This one is to make you more aware of your tactile sense. Gather a number of household items with different textures, like a moist sponge, a pair of pliers, bread soaked in cream soda, a razor blade, coffee grounds, two or three cockroaches, phlegm, and so forth. Dim the lights. Sit on a comfortable chair, blindfold yourself, and *slowly and gently* run your hands over the objects. Let the special texture of each imprint itself on your fingertips.

Now sit back and re-create in your mind the way each object felt. Recall the cold, chitinous backs of the roaches and their tiny flailing legs. Remember the cool slime of the phlegm, the unexpected slice of the razor. You'll be surprised at your tactile memory.

Touch everything one more time and go drink a glass of seltzer. Rest.

MASCULINITY EXERCISE NUMBER 2   One of the most important parts of your body for lovemaking is your tongue. It should be strong, strong, strong. To increase the strength of this vital erotic implement, ram it ten times into a tumbler of BBs or driveway gravel nightly before going to bed. When your tongue can pierce five thicknesses of shirt cardboard, it is a he-man tongue.

MASCULINITY EXERCISE NUMBER 3   Size of member *is* important. I strongly advise you to consult Charles Atlas' book *How to Mold a Mighty Dong*. His coexercises are excellent for adding those crucial few inches. One suggestion: if you cannot obtain a milking machine for Coexercise Number 7, try plugging it into your vacuum cleaner. The drapery-brush attachment is effective and quite pleasing to the touch.

MASCULINITY EXERCISE NUMBER 4   Go out and splurge on some really sexy underpants. It does wonders for your self-confidence to know that under your clothes you are wearing an elegantly wicked, transparent black bikini that makes you feel like Joe Namath about to visit Ann-Margret.

MASCULINITY EXERCISE NUMBER 5   This one is so important, I thought I had better devote a whole chapter to it. So keep reading and discover the importance of . . .

3. Whacking It

Yes, yes, I know. They say that if you play with it a little man will come and cut it off. The back of your head will collapse and you will go mad. It will lead to permanent sterility and death.

All quite true. Nonetheless, there is much to be learned from masturbatory workouts. What is your sensitivity-threshold index? Have you a uni- or multiple-estrus quotient? Can you hit the ceiling?

How many orgasms can you have in a single session? Some men are satisfied with one or two, others go as high as a quart. And, of course, some of you poor schmucks can't get it up at all. We'll solve *that* nagging problem now.

Erecting the Bell Tower

First, some definitions. The rounded head of your member is called the *German helmet,* after that peculiarly Teutonic headgear we all came to know so well during World War I and II. Beneath it is your *stalk,* then your *veldt,* then your *purse,* containing two *cojones* (co-HON-ase). Connecting *German helmet* to *stalk* is a vertical membrane called the *plynth.* And that small, grinning mouth in the center of your *German helmet* is your *slindle.*

Are you ready?

Pick a time when you are assured of privacy. Take your phone off the hook, turn down the lights, and whip it out. Yes, it's very ugly, but look at it anyway. Now touch it. Oh, come on, touch it. Hold it gently but firmly.

Slowly and sensually lubricate your *German helmet, plynth,* and *stalk* with any common household lubricant, such as baby oil or mayonnaise. Hum the "Theme from Victory at Sea" or some other romantic caprice. Is your cucumber getting ripe? It should be, but if it isn't, keep rubbing. DO NOT INSERT PENCILS OR OTHER LONG, THIN OBJECTS INTO YOUR SLINDLE. BE PATIENT.

Manipulation with Mechanical Devices

1. Vibrators can be seismic. The clerk in the drugstore may snigger at you, but up his. Used correctly, they could even raise a hard-on from my Uncle Durward, and he's dead!

2. The common home stereo system also proves to be deliciously exciting. Put on a Led Zeppelin album, jack up the bass response, and snuggle up against that woofer. Uhmmmm.

Manipulation with Animal Fats

Refer to any good cookbook to learn the process of larding. A friendly butcher can be a big help here.

Manipulation with Domestic Pets

1. Dogs can be trained to do anything. I have friends who are ecstatic about their canine experiences. Unfortunately, it is difficult if not impossible to untrain the dog when you wish to move on to members of your own species, and all too often the heartsick pooch must be shot.

2. Try sliding onto your erect member the liver-lined hub of a gerbil exercise wheel. You will find that these little fellows are tireless runners.

If, after all this, your member is still flaccid, slam a window on it. Women love a man in a cast.

4. Sex: Is It Evil?

It's taken us twenty centuries to get here, but the majority of people finally believe that sex between consenting partners is a natural and respectable part of an adult human being's life.

The joke's on them. Sex today is as immoral, lewd, sinful, and much fun as it ever was.

5. Making Her Think You're Cool

She'll never go for the real you, you understand. Inside, you are still a frightened little boy, making kaka in your pants. By skillful role-playing, however, you can make her *think* you're cool long enough to get into *her* pants.

Appearance

Luckily for you, she can't tell a book by its cover. Many a chewing gum has greatly increased its sales by adopting a colorful new wrapper, and if you want her to chew on yo' Wriggley, you'll do the same.

The art of appearance is complicated nowadays by the social imperative that your carefully contrived look seem accidental, or "real." A shortcut: dress as you normally would, stand under a shower for five minutes, let the wind of several fans dry you.

You'll be amazed at how fast and easy it is to walk away from your current look and step into another. All it takes is a little work and a total absence of integrity.

What to Say

The safest bet here is to be wishy-washy and noncommittal. Let her take the conversational lead, and you respond with comments such as "Far out" and "Too much." If you just don't disagree with her, she'll think you're on her side. Good. Soon you'll be handing her your weasel.

Cleanliness

Due to American phobia against reality, our women prefer men who are clean and unblemished.

Bathe often with soap containing an antibacterial agent, such as ammonia or lye. Then use a deodorant, an antiperspirant, a depilatory, and last of all, a fast-drying, unscented vinyl spray all over your entire body to "fix" you in your clean, pure state from the time you pick her up until you collapse from cell asphyxiation several hours later.

If your nose persists in dripping unsightly mucus, have it removed and invest in a plastoid-tin replacement.

Bloodshot eyes not only offend, they can get you arrested. If you can afford it, there are cosmetic surgeons who will permanently remove those tiny veins from your eyeballs. If not, you can find commercial salves that temporarily bleach redness while guaranteeing you at least 55 percent of your vision.

The Hazards of Sex

Venereal taint is the unsung fringe benefit of promiscuity. Syphilis and gonorrhea lend incredible status with the guys, and crabs, while publicly reviled, are really very cute and more loyal even than dogs.

6. Bedroom Threads

I'll bet you're one of those hamburgers who strides into the boudoir with nothing on but a hard and expects applause. If I were that woman, I'd throw vegetables at you.

What you wear to bed is important. Let's run down some of the classics.

An astonishing number of women are wild about leather jackets and cowboy boots. Others smack their lips and go into a carefree shuffle at the contrasting textures of feather boa and gun belt. I myself find this sort of thing garish, but if my woman climbs the bedpost and howls like a coyote at me in boots, I don't wait to grab a shoehorn.

Some women find a pair of glasses and a false moustache worn at the groin arousing.

Be imaginative. A hippie friend of mine decorated an old mailing tube with crayoned marihuana leaves, secured it about his member, and offered his old lady a toke. It drove her wild and she practically devoured him. Strangely enough, she also got high.

I think an example will illustrate just how important what you wear to bed can be.

Mark and Marylyn had been married three years. Until recently, Marylyn was beserk about Mark in bed. Then he noticed that slowly, almost imperceptibly, her interest was ebbing. No longer did she steal up behind him as he worked at his typewriter (he is a fisherman) and drape her breasts over his eyes. Gone were the days when she would work a sly finger up the back of the bum just as the elevator doors were closing. What was happening to his marriage?

When Marylyn announced she was leaving for two weeks to "sit at the bedside of a dying old friend," Mark knew he was in trouble. While she was away, he worked like a fiend. He went to Mr. Sampson's Emporium and purchased a Little Richard wig. He replaced his fingernails with tiny mirrors. He had his traditional bedroom done over as the cockpit of a B-17 and replaced their Louis XV bed with a leather hot-dog bun.

The day Marylyn was due back, Mark called her. He said that he would be tired when she got home and would she please humor him and follow exactly all the notes he would leave for her.

Utterly disinterested, Marylyn agreed. Unknown to Mark, she really was sitting with a dying old friend, and that unfortunate was even then in his terminal throes. Tired and depressed, she took a train home to New York.

She waited at the station for a half hour before remembering that her husband would not be picking her up. A few minutes later, she was told about the taxi and transit strikes. It took her an hour to walk home. When she arrived, there was a note on the door. It read: "The fact that you're home makes my *cojones* tingle. Put your suitcase down and go straight to the refrigerator."

Marylyn had left the suitcases on Seventeenth Street. Numbly she went into the kitchen. The note on the refrigerator door said: "Open me and you will find a very cold dry martini. Take it to the bathroom with you."

In the bathroom, she found the bath had been drawn. Gratefully, she slipped out of her clothes and into the tub. The water was cold as ice. Angry and shivering, she leaped out and grabbed a towel. The note taped to it said: "You have the most exciting body I have ever seen. I wish to bury my face in your Mountain of Venus. Come to the bedroom."

Marylyn went to the bedroom. As her bewildered eyes gradually adjusted to the soft green glow of the control panel, she made out Mark, attired in a striking black umpire suit, stretched out sensually in the hot-dog bun, stroking his unencumbered member with a pigeon feather and making soft cooing noises at her. Did she flip out! She pulled her pistol from the drawer of the night table and shot him in the chest!

Now here's where you'll be able to see just how important close attention to the details of bedroom dress can be. If Mark hadn't been carrying the "Rules of Baseball" in his breast pocket, the bullet would have pierced his heart!

Another ingenious clothing ploy was invented by my friend Benny. He and his wife were invited to an elegant party. Benny looked splendid in his midnight-blue tuxedo and patent-leather shoes. He dropped the bombshell just as the hostess was answering the door.

"My God, honey," he whispered. "In all the rush, I forgot to put on my underwear!"

"In your case, who'd notice?" replied his wife in a loud voice.

7. How to Tell in Advance if She'll Be Good in Bed

Without knowing it, she'll give you a number of clues.

Facial expressions can be very revealing. Does she eye your crotch and lick her lips noisily? That's a good sign.

When you introduce yourself by pressing her breast with your index finger and saying, "Honk honk," does she give you a dirty look and walk away? She's probably a lesbian.

Notice her kissing style. Is she a peaches, a prunes, or a banana?

Finally, the manner in which she touches your maleness is a dead giveaway. If she strokes it like a Siamese cat, you're hittin' on eight. If she acts as if she's starting a lawn mower, tell her to leave.

Now that you've decided *she'll* be good in bed, what about you? Well, hold on to your hats, turn the page, and find out . . .

8. How to Drive a Woman to Ecstasy

It's really quite simple. Take the Taconic State Parkway to the second Hillsdale exit, follow Route 110 north, turn left at the first crossroad after Mike's Shell Station, and you're there.

Now if it's fucking you're interested in, that's different. First, don't be afraid. Even sawdust has a sex life. Did you know that? I'm not sure it has a *great* sex life, but you never see bare floors in a wood shop.

Am I going to tell you to do some pretty wild things?

Uhmmhmmmm. I am going to tell you *exactly* how to perform the most wanton, degenerate acts I have ever heard of.

And, if you're as stupid as I think you are, you'll try every one of them.

Still game? Attaboy. Let's go.

WOMEN'S EROGENOUS ZONES

Women, like frying pans, have to be gotten hot before you put the meat in. To turn her on like a real masculine he-man, you have to know the territory. Most men don't realize that a woman's body is positively stippled with potential liver spots of erotic response.

Many women are surprised to find that out too.

For instance, did you know that the merest touch of a lit cigarette to her snatch will cause her to scream your name and writhe for minutes?

And that if you suspend her by her pinky toes, her eyeballs could fall out?

And that if you bit her softly on the buttocks, she may shit in your face?

Every woman is a sexual original. Not until you have explored every inch of her body, with X rays and proctoscope if necessary, will you truly know her.

But let's start at the beginning.

The Head

Here we mean exciting her erotically *inside* her head. This does not refer to squirting vinegar up her nostrils, but to the art of *suggestion*.

My friend Robbie called his wife Beverly one day during his lunch hour and told her just exactly what he had planned for her that night. His stratagem bore quick fruit; Beverly became so aroused that she inserted the receiver into her willie.

That night Robbie found her that way, quite insensate, tiny mewing emergency sirens echoing beneath her skirt. He strove for an hour to pluck this black plastic intruder from his wife's loins, but to no avail. Finally, he straightened and said, "Sorry, honey, no night of wild abandon tonight, I guess."

"Fuck off, small stuff," moaned Beverly in reply.

Visual aides, too, can make her feel very sexy. Did you know that French postcards appeal to many women? How they get aroused by looking at the Louvre and the Champs-Élysées is beyond me, but women will surprise you.

The Lips

The secret of good kissing is a slack jaw. If you've ever watched someone who is really retarded, you have the idea. Let your lips go completely limp. Don't worry: that strand of drool will only enhance the effect.

Now she will be irresistibly drawn to meet your lips with hers. Remembering Masculinity Exercise Number 2, thrust your he-man tongue deep into her mouth, taking care not to crush her uvula. When you have gone deep enough to make her gag, ease up and reverse. Repeat several times.

Vary your approach now and again. Lap the front of her face in upward swipes, occasionally darting the tip of your tongue into her nostril. Let her think you are about to kiss her mouth again, and when she closes her eyes, slip an uncooked wiener between her lips instead. Uhmmmm, how delicious.

Now run that tongue of yours down her cheek, into the shadowed hollows of her neck, three times around her breast, along her arm and onto the bedpost, across the wall to the far window, down its smooth pane, and into the grill of the air-conditioner. Could any woman resist?

The Breasts

Ah, knockers.

I tell you, I think that if I were in a flash fire and my date went all to pieces and I only had time to snatch one item per hand before fleeing to safety, I'd save the breasts.

If I were in Central Park and it were suddenly to *rain* breasts, my response, in sharp contrast to the disorientation of most strollers, would be to search for a bushel basket.

Breasts are wonderful!

Mammary fondles may be categorized as *squeezes, cuppings, bounces,* and *twists.* The last of these, incidentally, causes cancer.

Nipple erectors include the *palm-stroke, finger-flick, tongue-twit,* and *nasal-snuggie.* Take your time and be patient, but if, after five minutes or so, her pips remain stubbornly soft, affix an alligator clip to each and watch the fireworks.

Many men are confused about how to handle really *big* tits. What, they ask, does one *do* with all that bosom? Well, lift them. Swing them. Twirl and kiss and hug them. Pull them apart and let them crash together like church bells. Photograph them. Bury your face in the interbreast slick that inevitably forms. Rest them on a bureau top. Glove them in Baggies. Watch them float in the tub. Anything, Jim, anything!

The Buttocks

Yes, the buttocks: seat of her excretory portal and butt of a million bum jokes. Am I going to tell you hams how to make her popo rear with anticipation before you shoot the moon? Tush! Get to the bottom of *this* one yourselves.

The Virginia

And so, Big Casino. We come at last to the virginia, the honeypot at the end of her rainbow. Pat her legs and fix your gaze at the juncture of her thighs. You will see what appears to be a clam in a fright wig. See it glisten! But don't be drawn inside *quite* yet, for first we must pause to examine ...

YOUR WEE-WEE: A SKILLFUL MUSCLE

I had my first erection in the sixth grade as we sat in reading circle, discussing *Pongchoul, You Rascal.* Naturally I was mortified and held my loose-leaf notebook rigidly in my lap for the rest of the afternoon.

Ah, youth.

In my laters years, I was astonished to discover that my shameful bulge was the object of much admiration from the opposite sex, a fact I first suspected when three Puerto Rican streetwalkers accosted me on a late-night bus and, pointing to my groin, made wet, sucking noises through their teeth. My suspicions were confirmed when a female acquaintance admitted that, after noticing the provocative balloon in my bathing suit the previous summer, she had dreamed for three months of eating moray eel.

If women find it irresistible under wraps, do you think they go ape when you hang it out? In spades! But merely to dangle is tedious. Imagine if Oliver J. Dragon just hung limply over the stage; that wouldn't keep Fran interested for long, would it? Well, the same applies in the boudoir.

Learn to swing your member in circles. Lean your shoulders back against the wall, rotating your hips first to the left, then to the right. When you have mastered these simple circular moves, try figure eights, obelisks, tesseracts. Now—this is the difficult part—without letting it fall, bring it to instant hardness so that it stands in a zingy, vibrating salute. Got it? Good, you're doing very well.

Now, when you enter her, you want her to pulsate and

throb and hunger for you in scarlet shades, rising in pitch and tempo until she feels as if forty-three suns have just gone nova in the center of her maddened virginia.

That takes muscle.

Refer to the Charles Atlas book for appropriate coexercises. When you can lift both her feet off the floor by penal flex alone, she's getting the hang of it.

What do you get out of this? Three things: (1) the knowledge that you're probably hurting her, (2) almost certain hernia, and (3) a good shot at the Tom Snyder show.

So develop those penals and phalloids. And remember that a masculine he-man must also be able to excel at . . .

EATING IT RAW

Scared, huh? Quite understandable. All the guys are scared the first few times. I mean, we all know what comes out of there, right? But, then, you probably didn't like your first taste of beer either. Oral sex is part of the total bundle of degeneracies you have to offer, which is about *all* you have to offer, so you better know what you're doing.

Does the idea of putting a woman's cupcake in your mouth bother you? If so, you are a typical product of this nation's foolish taboos against sidewalk fish markets. But, actually, kissing her between her legs is a lot less unsanitary than kissing your pet's litter box. And, as for oral sex being "wrong," you'll just have to get used to it.

The first time a woman "went down on me," I struck her. I was, frankly, a little shocked. "Where were you brought up," I asked her, "in a barn?" Apparently she got the message, for, much to my relief, she snatched up her clothes and ran from the room crying. Later, however, when I learned that oral sex was all the rage among decaying Balkan aristocrats, I changed my tune fast. Here are a few basic techniques I learned.

Setting the Stage Have her lie on her back, legs slightly spread. Bring your ear to the mouth of her virginia. Can you hear the sea? Good. Now turn face forward and shout, "AAAAHRRRRRRRR." Her *lablia majorca* will open, revealing her *vestibule*. If it is late morning, you may see the postman sorting letters into their proper boxes. If so, politely ask him to leave. Most letter carriers are good fellows and quickly comply. Now you are ready for stylistic niceties.

Rootin' for Taters This technique emphasizes thrust and depth. Can you touch her liver? Her lung?

The Marlon Press your mouth firmly against her cookie and make loud Harley-Davidson noises. Go through all four gears, brake, and peel out from a standing start. Continue this sequence until she tells you to stop acting like an idiot.

The Hindenburg Maintaining a tight seal, expel your breath into her until she has inflated to three or four times her original size. Release her and watch her jet crazily about the room.

After all this, she will be close to orgasm. I know some men who believe that women "come," as men do. This is not true. However, many a woman's *lablia* will, as she peaks, snap together audibly. Be ready to move fast; I have a friend, Tim, who lost the tip of his nose in this fashion.

Are you still with me? You may not be for long, because now it's time to stick it . . .

UP THE COAL SHUTE

Decadent former Waffen SS swear by this one. If you must do it, at least avert your eyes. Preferably, take careful aim with your crazed kielbasa and slide into . . .

HOME PLATE

It's taken you months of anxiety, thousands of tongue thrusts, untold coexercises, and a single-mindedness bordering on obsession, but you are finally experiencing the most pleasurable and fulfilling love act known to man. Congratulations!

Yes, it *is* kind of a letdown, isn't it?

9. After the Bed, Where?

Women are adventuresome. They soon tire of the bedroom and wish to experiment with daring and offbeat sexual locales. Be excited! Sex is about to take on whole new dimensions for you.

Since I started following my women's whims, I've made love in a deserted piano (very nice), on an ironing board (rickety), inside a rolltop desk (close), in a thresher (scary), in a roaring fire (ouch!), and hundreds of other places I'd be embarrassed to mention.

Naturally, don't follow her just anywhere. Remember Beverly, the telephone girl? Apparently hung up on the erotic possibilities of modern conveniences, she enticed Robbie one Sunday afternoon into making love in the incinerator shaft, and, of course, that was the end of them. Have fun, but use common sense.

10. Should You Talk?

Oh, sho'.

But don't forget that women are more romantic than men. "Do the Philly dog, now" is *not* what she wants to hear. Rather, speak softly and let your words crawl like snails into her ears.

Incidentally, a friend told me one day that it didn't matter what words you said, as long as you said them romantically. I was intrigued. That night, I huskily whispered to my lover the names of several common fruits and vegetables. It worked like a charm. She pulled free of my embrace, strode to the kitchen, and made herself a salad.

11. Women's Sexual Fantasies

Whew, did I have a hard time getting women to talk about this one! My knuckles were bleeding and raw by the time I forced out these four fantasies. I offer them for what they're worth, which probably isn't much.

Fantasy Number 1 While you're making love to her, she has her eyes closed and is pretending you're a man.

Fantasy Number 2 She has fallen from a window near the top of the Chrysler Building and is plummeting toward the sidewalk. Down below, you espy her, and thinking fast, you wheel a nearby fruit-car directly beneath her line of fall. She lands with a squish, unharmed. Grateful, she begins licking the fruit pulp from you, until, unable to stand it any longer, you tear off your clothes and dive in on top of her. You make love as the fruit vendor berates you in broken English.

Fantasy Number 3 This one is common. At least two, and

sometimes as many as five or six, soldiers of varying races, colors, and creeds make love to her simultaneously. Sometimes this occurs in a mess hall, other times in an armory.

Fantasy Number 4   Just as you are about to enter her, your member turns into a hungry boa constrictor. It plunges into her and roars through her innards like an express train, devouring everything. Frightened, she assumes the form of a mongoose and pecks out your eyes.

12. The Sense of Glut

And so, at last, you fall back exhausted. The time has come for you to put down your pud, pull up your pants, and go out to meet some women. They're out there by the thousands, waiting for you to drown them with passion and other substances, and if you've read this book *carefully,* if you've put your *trust* in me, you're a bigger fool than I thought you were.

And now, if you'll excuse me, I'm going out to warm up the car and drive *my* woman to Ecstasy. VRRRUH-MMMMM

On the Night Before the Last Day They Filmed Star Trek

But for a single feature, Dorcas 8 would have been the least inviting planet yet discovered by man. Her surface was a global sea of stagnant blue mud that clashed horribly with her lemon-yellow sky and continuously blurped up lazy mile-wide bubbles whose bursting loosed a scent that rivaled the mating ichor of the Arcturan phlegm-toad. Certainly this depressing world and its dour inhabitants—a race of squat, plum-colored frog beings—would have been passed over entirely by the human race were it not for the special properties of her polar regions. Here, over small radii, she had "frozen" to a curious pseudo-solid that had proved to contain a subsurface fungus called *Truffle aphroditis*, and here, therefore, Starfleet Command had dispatched the starship *Enterprise* to fetch several tons of this vitally important material for dispersal among certain highly placed friends in the Bureau-cratic-Industrial Complex of Earth.

Captain Kirk felt relieved when the Dorcan work party hauled the final sledgeload of sealed freeze-canisters to the beam-up-point. Transport these to the *Enterprise* and he could collect the members of his detail and get the hell out of here. Dorcas 8 gave him the creeps. He flipped open his communicator, gave an order, and watched with satisfaction as the canisters shimmered and vanished. The Dorcan miners had already received their payment; most of them now headed for the bawdy houses among the nearby tumble of shacks that composed this planet's largest "city." Repressing a shudder of distaste, Kirk put his hands to his mouth and called, "Scotty! Sulu! Chekov! Let's go!"

Lieutenant Sulu and Ensign Chekov emerged obligingly from an edge of the shantytown and jogged to Kirk's side. As they came to attention, he noted on their faces expressions that were slightly too innocent.

"Well, gentlemen. Where's Mr. Scott?"

Sulu and Chekov exchanged blank looks.

"Mr. Scott, sir? Ve thought he vas vith you, sir," said Chekov.

Since Kirk was standing in the midst of a flat, empty clearing, obviously alone, he accepted this answer with some reservations. He repeated his question to the remaining pair of Dorcan miners, who were loitering a few yards distant, eyeing the Terrans curiously. They convulsed in sudden croaking laughter, puffing their throat sacs in delight, and hopped rapidly away. Kirk was beginning to grow angry.

"Lieutenant, I'm not asking again. Where is Mr. Scott?"

Sulu cast a glance at Chekov, but the ensign's attention seemed riveted on a largish bubble swelling on the left horizon. Swallowing, he turned back to Kirk.

"Well, sir, you know how Scotty—that is, Mr. Scott, sir—how he never takes leave on any of the planets where we stop, how he spends all his leave time in the ship's library reading technical manuals?"

Kirk nodded impatiently.

"Well, uh, Ensign Chekov and I were talking the other night and we found ourselves wondering ..." Sulu was sweating. He appeared to be having difficulty finishing.

"Yes?"

"... wondering, sir, whether Mr. Scott had ever ..." He broke off, flapped his mouth soundlessly twice, and turned beseechingly to Chekov.

"... ever had *relations*, Captain," Chekov finished for him, and nodded, as if in agreement with himself.

"What are you two talking about? What have you done with Mr. Scott?"

Chekov stepped closer and spoke conspiratorially.

"Ve got him laid, sir."

"Laid?" Kirk was aghast. "Laid? Laid by whom?"

"You mean by *what*, sir," said Sulu.

"Are you telling me you brought Mr. Scott, my chief engineer, to a Dorcan female, a froglike alien, to get him *laid?*"

"That's right, sir," said Chekov brightly.

"Well, let's go get him then, gentlemen. We want to get out of here, don't we?"

Uncomfortable silence.

"I'm afraid ve can't go get him, sir. He's been eaten."

"What? You mean Scotty actually submitted to an act of fell—?"

"No, sir, I mean he vas eaten. It turns out that Dorcans are carnivorous, sir."

Kirk could scarcely believe his ears. Scotty—eaten? "Lieutenant, Ensign, consider yourselves confined to quarters." He flipped open his communicator. "Kirk here. Security team to the transporter room. Beam us up."

The transporter caught them in its field, prickling Kirk's skin a bit more than usual, he thought.

He had scarcely remanded his two junior officers to custody when he received a call from the bridge.

"Spock here, Captain. I'm afraid I have some bad news for you. In your absence, Engineering reported the disappearance of our entire supply of dilithium crystals."

Kirk was staggered. Without dilithium crystals, the great engines of the *Enterprise* were so much junk. He and his crew were stranded in orbit around a miserable blue mudball, seventeen thousand light-years from home. This on top of the loss of his chief engineer. He felt suddenly the need for a shot of Saurian brandy.

"Spock, do what you can. I'll meet you on the bridge in ten minutes. Kirk out."

He turned from the wall grid and walked rapidly to Dr. McCoy's medical complex. His head throbbed dully.

"Bones," he called, "everything's gone wrong. Scotty's dead, Sulu and Chekov are acting insane, and our entire dilithium crystal supply has vanished."

McCoy entered from his inner lab. "And you thought a nice shot of Saurian brandy might help, I'll bet. Well, fine. In fact, I prescribe it." He poured a shot of the ruby liquor and passed it to Kirk with a wink.

"Bones, thanks." Kirk downed it, felt grateful for the small fireball it made in his belly. "Now, about Sulu and—"

"Way ahead of you, Jim boy. Those two've been acting strange for a few days now. I think I've synthesized the curative serum. Come have a look."

Kirk followed him into the rear lab. On the far wall, hanging by her wrists from a pair of brackets, was Nurse Chapel. She was nude.

"Bones, what . . ."

"Yes, I'm proud of her too, Jim. Christine is donating a vital ingredient to that serum I just mentioned. Aren't you, honey?" He reached up and titillated her labia with a medical tool.

"Marrghhh! Leonard, Leonard, you Svengali," moaned

Nurse Chapel, and several droplets of bright, clear liquid winked from her interior to plop into a Florence flask affixed between her thighs by an arrangement of clamps. McCoy pulled the flask free and held it up for inspection.

"See, Jim? Essence de Low Tide!"

Kirk strode rapidly to a wall grid. "Security to Dr. McCoy's laboratory, on the double."

Dr. McCoy began to laugh.

After the doctor was led away, Kirk half-ran to an elevator. He wanted the solidity of Spock, needed his counsel. But when he arrived on the bridge, he found it deserted but for Lieutenant Uhura.

"Where is everybody? Where's Spock?"

"Ah don' know, Cappin. When Missuh Spock say you wuz comin' up, dey all start laughin'. Den dey run out an' Spock go chasin' after dem."

Kirk rolled his eyes helplessly. "What is going *on* around here? Lieutenant, contact Starfleet immediately. I need help." He took his captain's chair.

He felt numbed by the recent sequence of events, too dispirited even to make a log entry. He didn't notice Uhura standing quietly beside him for several moments.

"Oh, Lieutenant. You've reached Starfleet?"

"Yassuh, Cappin, Ah got an open channel on de receiver mah daddy give me." She lifted her uniform skirt and thrust her nether Afro at Kirk, spreading herself open with the fingers of both hands. From within, a tiny voice called, "Kirk, are you there? This is Starfleet Command calling the *Enterprise*. Have we been cut off?"

Kirk could find no words. "Here, Cappin," purred Uhura, mounting his chair and pushing her pud close to his face. Just then, the elevator doors whisked open and Spock strode briskly onto the bridge.

"Captain?" He raised an eyebrow.

"Spock! Am I ever glad to see you! Listen, we've got to—Lieutenant, *will* you get off me?—do something! The whole crew's gone crazy!"

"Yes, sir. I believe I have isolated the cause. It appears that after you beamed down alone to the planet, Mr. Scott and Dr. McCoy removed about a third of the dilithium crystals and snorted them."

"They *snorted* our dilithium crystals?"

"That is correct, Captain. They seemed pleased at the physiological consequences and made an aerosol of the remaining crystals, which they disseminated through the ship's ventilators some minutes before Scott and the others joined you on the planet's surface." He paused. "Naturally, as a Vulcan, I was unaffected."

"Spock, will *I* be affected?"

"Yes, sir, you will. But I believe I have found an antidote for you. On Vulcan, it has long been known that many forms of mental imbalance can be easily cured by the ingestion of certain internal fluids of Terran females. In fact, before your world and mine established diplomatic contact, Vulcans occasionally appeared on Earth in what your ancestors called "flying saucers" and removed a female or two. Remember Amelia Earhart? But I digress. I suggest you allow Lieutenant Uhura to help you."

He sat Kirk back down and motioned to the comely communications officer, who eagerly reattained Kirk's chair arms, squatted, and drew his face into the musky dimness of her chocolate parfait.

"Eat, Captain, you'll feel better," came Spock's distant voice.

Shrugging, Kirk began to eat. He'd barely begun, however, when he felt the lieutenant's brimming muzzle pulled rudely away. He opened his eyes to find Scotty, Sulu, Chekov, McCoy, Nurse Chapel, and Spock arraying before him, grinning and nudging one another.

"I think we can stop this little charade right here, Captain," said Spock.

"What are you talking about?" asked Kirk, bewildered. "Why?"

"Because, Jim," chanted his crew in unison, "this is the Old Dream Ending!"

And when Gene Roddenberry woke up, he found several mouthfuls missing from his mattress.

SIGNET Humor Books You'll Want to Read